Following God
for YOUTH
and young adults

VICE VERSA

Breaking through from
Old to New

A STUDENT BIBLE STUDY, ideal for small groups

by
David Rhodes, Chad Norris, and Chris Brooks

✤ AMG Publishers

Following God:
VICE VERSA Student Devotional Guide

Copyright © 2005 Wayfarer Ministries, Inc.

Published by AMG Publishers.

ISBN 0-89957-742-3

First printing: April 2005

Edited by: Robert Neely and Rick Steele

Interior Layout: Rick Steele

Cover design and interior design elements: Daryl Phillips and Jeff Belk at ImageWright Marketing and Design, Chattanooga, TN

Special thanks: David Reichley, Jennifer Johnsey

Wayfarer Ministries
116 Hidden Hill Road
Spartanburg, SC 29301
864-587-4985

Printed in the United States of America

10 09 08 07 06 05 -C- 6 5 4 3 2
web sites: www.wayfarerministries.org   www.amgpublishers.com

to the engage community

Table of Contents

VICE VERSA

Welcome to the journey of *Vice Versa*. We hope you begin this eight-week journey with the attitude necessary for any Bible study to be successful: willingness to honestly evaluate your own life and openness to encounter God's message through Scripture, prayer, meditation, and the other avenues that we've included in this journey. If you've studied with us before, we hope you've found us to be honest people asking tough questions and looking for the light of Scripture to shine through on every page. If you're picking up a Following God for Youth study for the first time, let us make this commitment to you from the outset: We will do our best in this study to be honest, to ask real questions about God and what he is trying to say to us , and to make each day connect to your daily life. We the authors are not superhero saints with answers to every question or people who never struggle or make bad decisions. We are normal people who are passionate about a journey to know God and discover real life.

So why did we write *Vice Versa*? To be honest, the reason we have written this study is that no one ever presented these concepts to us in this fashion. Sure, we were told to avoid sin, but we were rarely pushed to embrace a new kind of life-the life God created us to live, one of freedom, joy, and constant "newness." Why the title *Vice Versa*? Because the world is a tough place to follow God, and crossroads that lead either to life as God intends or life that is less than God's best are around every corner. Because often, the way to the best life looks like death at first glance, and the road to death often looks like life at first. If we are left on this journey alone, we will too often travel the wrong road for miles only to discover that we are off course or at a dead end. Because too many of us as Christians find ourselves more enslaved to sin than free in Christ, and because the world needs Christians who do more than avoid sin—it needs Christians who discover real life and live it to the full.

So we invite you on this journey into freedom. This book doesn't try to give seven steps to a sin-free life; instead, it presents an honest approach concerning our struggle with sin, and it presents a picture of the freedom God offers. We believe the best way to break free of sin is to whet your appetite for something different. That's what this book is all about. We won't promise to answer all your questions or even attempt to do so, but we hope and pray that this book will point you in a new direction. Let the journey begin.

David Rhodes, Chad Norris, and Chris Brooks

Tips...

This student devotional book is intended to help you journey with Christ as you seek to put off vices and live in the freedom for which God created you.

Some of you are working through this study on your own, and some of you are going through this study in a group. Either way, this book is designed to take truths about God and help you understand them, experience them and apply them to your daily life. Our hope is that, if you've gone through the devotions in the week leading up to your group time, you will be able to share your thoughts with the group and build on the things you learned during the week during that time. If you are going through this study on your own, we hope that you will take some time to enter into discussions with your friends, family and ministers about the things you are learning.

The book is divided into eight lessons with the purpose of allowing the reader to do one lesson per week for eight weeks. There are five devotional readings for each week's lesson. Although we have divided the devotions according to the five-day schedule, feel free to create your own schedule for completing your study.

Recognizing that there is no perfect structure for time alone with God, we have tried to produce devotions that are both varied and consistent. This book provides stories, questions, illustrations, background information, charts, and other tools to help illuminate the featured Scripture for each day and encourage and challenge your view of God.

Finally, at the end of each week, there is a notes page, which we hope you will use to take notes during your group session if you are going through *Vice Versa* with others or to journal your own personal highlights from the week if you are going through the study on your own.

We believe this study will help you break through from old to new. Let the journey begin.

WEEK ONE

from pride to humility
(there is a God, and i'm not him)

super
sized

When I was a kid, few things in life were better than going to McDonald's.® After climbing through the playground and smelling the hamburgers and french fries, my friends and I imagined that heaven was decorated with golden arches. The climax of the McDonald's experience was the moment I got my hands on the Happy Meal.® This lunch box had everything a kid could want: a hamburger (or chicken nuggets if you preferred), fries, a small drink, and of course the thing that made a Happy Meal so happy—the prize.

For years, I ordered a Happy Meal every time I went to McDonald's, and I loved it every time. I had no idea that there was anything else on the menu. I had seen my parents eat some things at McDonald's that I never found in my Happy Meal box, but I thought those options weren't available to kids. That's why I've never forgotten the day my Happy Meal world was shattered.

I think I was seventeen when I discovered Big Macs® and super-size fries thanks to my grandfather. (OK, maybe I wasn't 17, but I was pretty old, because my parents kept me on Happy Meals as long as they could to protect the family budget.) In the middle of a day fishing with my father, my brother, and my Papa, we went to McDonald's for lunch. Papa said some words I'll never forget: "I'm paying. You can order anything you want." For the first time, I looked at the menu and saw exotic offerings like Quarter Pounders with Cheese® and the Filet-o-fish,® and they became real to me. The super-size fries and extra-large drink I got with the No. 1 value meal I ordered dwarfed what I had always received with the Happy Meal. And to be honest, while sometimes I miss getting the prize, I have never gone back to ordering Happy Meals.

Read Daniel 4

- Which best describes Nebuchadnezzar's view of God in verses 4-30?
  - ❑ Happy Meal
  - ❑ super-sized

- **Which best describes Nebuchadnezzar's view of God in verses 31-37?**

  - ❑ Happy Meal
  - ❑ super-sized

If life is all about climbing the ladder, being the man (or woman), and being the most popular, then Nebuchadnezzar had it made. He was the most powerful man in the most powerful nation of his day. In fact, he was so powerful that all his power went to his head. He thought life was all about him, his credit, and his glory. That's why Nebuchadnezzar is the perfect person to look at as we open our study of *Vice Versa*. He was proud, and pride and self-centeredness are at the heart of every sin. But Nebuchadnezzar had an experience with God—one like something out of a science-fiction movie—that let him know who God truly is. Once Nebuchadnezzar saw God as he truly is, his life would never be the same.

Our world today tells us that life is all about us, and we have become Nebuchadnezzars of sorts. Still, with all of us acting like we are God, we find ourselves becoming less and less free. That's why Nebuchadnezzar's awakening (and ours) to the truth that **there's a God, and I'm not him**, is so important. As long as we think of God as a Happy Meal-sized being who gives out prizes, pride is possible. But when we awaken to our super-sized God, we really begin to understand who God is and in turn who we are. This is the crucial first step on the journey from vices to freedom and particularly on the path from pride to humility.

- **How has your view of God and life been Happy Meal-sized in the past?**

_____

_____

_____

_____

_____

■ How has your view of God grown in the
past? Explain those situations.

_____

_____

_____

_____

_____

_____

■ Where in your life now do you have a
Happy Meal-sized view of God?

_____

_____

_____

■ What would it take for you to see God
as he really is?

_____

_____

_____

Ask God to show you how he is super-sized in this study and in your life.

treasure
or trash

When I was growing up, my family had a dog named Dusty. I know Dusty is not an original name for a dog, but everyone else in my family had names beginning with D, so we thought the dog should too. Dusty was a good dog, other than his magnetism for fleas, his table manners, and his tendency to run off, especially when we were in a hurry to get somewhere. He was fun to play with and snuggle with, and he was always good for a laugh.

Dusty loved to eat "people food." Somewhere along the way, he was fed from the table, and once he tasted what we were eating, his Alpo wasn't very appealing to him anymore. Memories of meals at my house feature the members of my family sitting around the table and Dusty's head bobbing up at the corner, looking to see what was for dinner. Dusty whined and was never satisfied until he got some of our dinner.

One night, Dusty's hunger got the best of him. Mom had cooked a turkey that evening, filling the house with the type of aroma that normally only came at Thanksgiving and Christmas. Dusty got some turkey for dinner, but I guess the smell was more than he could bear, because at 3 a.m. the entire family was awakened by terrible sounds of pain coming from the kitchen. We all ran downstairs to find Dusty lying on his back, covered in grease, and the turkey carcass pulled out of the trash, picked clean of any meat. Dusty hadn't just eaten the turkey; it looked like he had bathed in it.

I've often thought back to that night and wondered what was going through Dusty's mind. He had to think we were holding out on him and trying to make him miserable by not giving him all the turkey he could handle or allowing him to pick the bones clean. So he decided to take matters into his own paws—and once he did, there was no turning back. And in the end, the decision that Dusty thought would bring him more pleasure and more freedom brought him the worst stomach pain of his life.

Read Genesis 3:1-13

- What did Adam and Eve do wrong in this chapter?
  - ❏ touched the tree of the knowledge of good and evil
  - ❏ ate fruit from the tree of knowledge of good and evil
  - ❏ planted the tree of the knowledge of good and evil

(You may want to look at Genesis 2:17 before you answer, because what God really said and Eve's version are different.)

- What did the serpent tell Eve would happen if she ate the fruit?

_____

_____

Dusty's turkey dinner helps me understand what must have been going on in the hearts of Adam and Eve when they sinned against God. The serpent convinced them that God was holding out on them, and as a result they were no longer content to be made in God's image. They wanted to be "like" God—or, more honestly, to be God. But their choice to eat the fruit did not turn out the way they planned or the way the serpent promised. Instead of finding freedom, they found themselves hiding in the bushes in fear of God, their innocence compromised and their world broken. As in Dusty's case, there were consequences to their actions.

The truth is, you and I wouldn't make very good gods. We think we would be more free if we were in charge, but every time I take my life in my own hands, I come away disappointed. Sure, at first things may seem better, but the further I get down the road of serving myself and trying to become my own god, the more I realize that I'm not very good at it. That's because I was never meant to be a god, and neither were you. There is only one God; it's not me, and it's not you either.

When we let God place his value on us instead of trying to be him ourselves, we can become truly free. God's not holding out on us. He does really have our best interests at heart. Pride tells us that we are our own gods, but humility accepts our position as made in God's image and trusts that freedom comes from finding our identity under God's authority.

- Have you ever made a decision that you thought would make you freer only to find yourself with less freedom later?
    - ❏ yes
    - ❏ no

If so, explain that situation.

_____

_____

_____

_____

prayer exercise:

Use the diagrams on the next page to reflect on your relationship with God. The first diagram pictures how we try to find our identity outside of or in competition with God. The other shows how we find our identity inside of God. Spend some time asking the Spirit to show you places in your life where you are trying to be God or find your identity outside of him. Ask him how you can find your identity in him. Write what God places on your heart around the diagram as a prayer.

Us vs. God

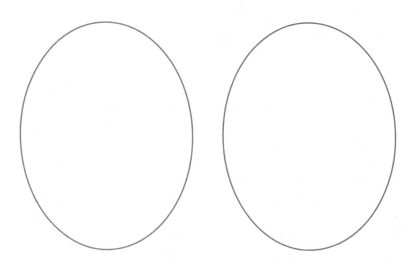

Us in God

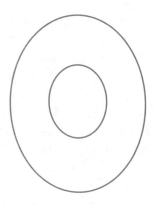

the pride
God hates

It happens all the time. Every time certain football players reach the end zone, they celebrate like crazy. And as the rest of us watch these celebrations, we have to ask ourselves whether we love them or hate them. No one can deny that end-zone celebrations in the National Football League have never been more noticeable. In fact, people often end up talking more about the celebrations than about the games. From Terrell Owens signing a football with a Sharpie® that he had tucked inside his sock, to Joe Horn faking a cell-phone call, to the variety of dances and actions other players do, it seems that there's a memorable celebration almost every week during the football season.

These celebrations can be entertaining, but they also make me think about pride, because they draw attention to the individual, not the team. The pride on display in the end zone makes it seem that the team concept is dead. In professional sports, pride seems to be the norm.

Read Luke 18:9-14

Fill in the blanks
Luke 18:9 says, "To some who were
_____ of their _____
_____ and looked _____ on
everybody else, Jesus told this parable."

Like any good communicator, Jesus had a target audience in mind when he told this story. It was a group of people that made Jesus furious throughout the gospels—the proud. Jesus showed little patience for the arrogant.

When you think about it, it's ridiculous for any of us to struggle with pride. A person characterized by arrogance has really lost sight of who God is. The best cure for pride is being in the presence of God. The more time you spend in his presence, the more you realize that God is bigger than you are, and the more you notice that pride is not part of God's character.

Jesus is humility in the flesh. Throughout the gospels, we see how our Savior came not to be served but to serve. He let the children come to him. He washed his disciples' feet. He gave his life as a sacrifice. When you think of this, it's no surprise that people were attracted to Jesus. The lost ran to him, but the prideful religious establishment had problems with him.

One of the biggest problems with Christianity today is that the world often sees Christians as prideful and arrogant. The truth is, they are right to think that way. The Christian religious establishment of our day often acts much like the Pharisees did in Jesus' day. This is a huge problem. If we are going to share Jesus with an unsaved world, then we need to become more like Jesus by getting rid of pride and growing in humility. Jesus isn't looking for more Pharisees; he's looking for people like the tax collector—and like himself—who are humble.

■ How does this parable make you feel?

❏ convicted   ❏ assured

❏ confused   ❏ thankful

■ With whom do you identify in this story?

❏ the Pharisee

❏ the tax collector

Why?

_____

_____

_____

_____

■ Why do you think the Lord loves the humble so much?

_____

_____

_____

_____

Spend some time reflecting on what you read today and ask yourself some tough questions. Are you more like the Pharisee, who was full of pride of arrogance, or are you like the tax collector, truly aware of your need for the Savior? Where are there pockets of pride in your life? Ask the Holy Spirit to show you places in your life that are marked by pride and use this time to confess these areas. Celebrate the humility of Christ by praising him for the person he is. Tell God how much you appreciate his humble example and ask him for the courage to walk in the same way.

the pride
God likes

■ Does God want us to ever brag or boast?

❑ yes

❑ no

Explain your answer.

_____

_____

_____

_____

_____

Life is full of things that are just plain odd. For example, why do we drive on a parkway and park on a driveway? Once, when I was driving, I saw a man standing on his head on top of a billboard. I guess he was trying to make a political statement or something, but the only statement that came to my mind is, "Man, is *that* strange."

The Bible is full of things that seem to be odd. The plagues in Egypt and Noah building a boat before it had ever rained are just two examples of this. But one of the oddest things in the Bible is something God told Jeremiah.

Read Jeremiah 9:23-24

■ Do you find it odd that God told his people to boast in something?

❑ yes

❑ no

Explain your answer.

- **Why would God want us to boast about something?**

_____

_____

_____

When I read the Bible, I consistently ask myself this question: "What does the Father call Christianity?" I'm tired of making Christianity what I want it to be. Jesus is looking for people to follow him on his and his Father's terms, and I want to be one of these people. I want to know him.

It's exciting when we begin to see who God truly is. Hebrews 1 tells us that Jesus reveals who the Father is. Jesus constantly told people who God is and what he is like. Even more, Jesus revealed what God is truly like with his life.

Jeremiah 9 foreshadows what Jesus wanted everyone to know. God wants us to know him. This is exactly what God told Jeremiah to tell people to boast in. If there is one thing in this world that we are supposed to take pride in, it is the fact that we know God. At its most basic level, Christianity is about truly knowing God. This is to be the pursuit of our lives.

The Old Testament was written in Hebrew, and the English word "know" in this passage is translated from the Hebrew _yada_. This word describes an intimate and close relationship. God is not saying that he wants us to know a lot about him. Instead, the Lord is saying that he wants us to know him intimately. He desires to walk with us in very close communion. God desires intimacy with us, and this passage tells us that we can boast and take pride in knowing him in this way.

- Do you know about God, or do you know him? Explain your answer.

_____

_____

_____

_____

- Why do you think God tells us to boast about knowing him? Why is this so important?

_____

_____

_____

_____

prayer exercise:

Take some time to talk to the Father about your desire to know him. Ask him how you can become a person who boasts about knowing him. Pour your heart out to him and tell him how you want to know him in this way. Ask him to show you what it means to "yada" or truly experience him as your Father.

freedom
in humility

■ What is your dream job?

_____

_____

■ Imagine applying for this dream job.
  What are five things that you think a
  potential employer would be looking
  for from a candidate?

_____

_____

_____

_____

_____

Many times, we treat being a Christian like it's a job. We try to build our
resumes with lots of good works so that God will like us—and so that we
can be proud that we deserve to be Christians. That's what was happening
in Philippi when Paul wrote and said that, although he had a great resume,
it wasn't what brought him freedom. Humility did.

Read Philippians 3:4-6

■ What did Paul say he could take pride
  in or have confidence in? (Check all
  that apply.)

  ❑ He was a Pharisee
  ❑ He was righteous and faultless

- ❑ He was good-looking
- ❑ He was an exemplary Jew
- ❑ He did his job well
- ❑ He was rich

■ What things are you tempted to take pride in?

_____

_____

_____

_____

Most of the things Paul said he could take pride in were good things, and they were sources of pride for many people in his day. But Paul went on to say that he found real freedom not in the things he could take pride in but in the things he could be humble about because of God.

Read Philippians 3:7-9

■ What did Paul say about the things he used to take pride in?

❑ verse 7: "I now consider _____ "
❑ verse 8: "I consider them _____

Pride leads us to try to earn everything we can so that we can brag about it, and it causes us to do good deeds in order to earn right standing with God. But Paul reminds us that righteousness does not come from anything we do; it comes from God himself. Humility leads us as Christians to be honest about who we really are—good, bad, and ugly—and allows us to celebrate what God has done in our lives to transform and redeem us. That's what Paul did in these verses, and it's what God wants us to do as well. Instead of seeking to earn our way into God's good graces, we can live in a way that humbly gives God thanks for saving and changing us. This is the way to freedom in humility.

prayer exercise:

Thank God for the freedom that humility brings. Ask him to show you ways that you're trying to earn his favor. As he does, tell him you're sorry for showing pride in these ways. Ask God to show you ways that you can live a life of thankful humility instead.

_____

_____

_____

_____

_____

_____

_____

_____

_____

_____

_____

_____

_____

This page is designed to give you space to take notes during your "Vice Versa" group session or to journal your reflections on the highlights of this week's study.

WEEK TWO

from lust to love
(finding love in a lust-filled world)

view
from the roof

When I was a teenager, my family went on vacation to Fernandina Beach, Florida. Like most kids, my brother and I wanted to find the biggest waves and bodysurf them as far as we could. We were in luck, because the day we arrived, a storm was coming in, and the waves were huge. My brother and I ran toward the water as quickly as we could, and we caught wave after wave.

After doing this for about an hour, we noticed that the waves were getting stronger and stronger. We thought about heading in, but we decided to stay out in the water a little longer. That was a huge mistake. About five minutes later, my brother and I caught a wave so strong that we were driven to the bottom of the ocean floor and trapped there for what seemed like an eternity. Finally, I was able to pop my head above the surface of the water. I scrambled to look for my 8-year-old brother and found him, crying and groggy. The wave had been so strong and the current so powerful that both of us almost drowned. It was one of the scariest moments of my life.

Read 2 Samuel 11

■ What is your reaction to this story?

❑ shocked   ❑ entertained
❑ scandalized   ❑ stunned
❑ saddened   ❑ other _____

Fill in the blanks
Second Samuel 11:27 says, "After the time of mourning was over, David had her brought to his house, and she became his wife and bore him a son. But the thing David had done _____ the _____."

King David loved God very much, and he wanted to please God and live his life for him. But David had a vice that should serve as a warning to all of us. As we see in this passage, lust got the best of him. King David became entangled by this sin, and it eventually led him to other sins of lying and even murder.

Lust leads us into bondage that none of us want. Fighting the struggle of lust is much like being trapped under a wave. This week, we'll look at the struggle with lust and the freedom that God offers. God is not content to leave us drowning in this sin; he wants us to experience the freedom to love. Let David's story resonate with you this week as we tackle this issue. David's sin led to drastic consequences, as we'll see tomorrow. But even in this, he found grace and continued to experience God in his life. His story shows us that no matter where you are in the struggle with lust, there is hope for you. God promises never to leave us or forsake us, whatever we are going through.

■ **What struggles with lust are you experiencing?**

_____

_____

_____

■ **Do you feel as though you can experience freedom in this area of your life?**
   ❏ **yes**
   ❏ **no**

Why or why not?

_____

_____

_____

_____

_____

Ask the Lord to help you hear him this week. Be open and honest with him about how lust influences your life. Give him the opportunity to work in you this week by taking time to spend with him.

the way
to destruction

It's a well-known science-fiction storyline, and it always creeps me out. Whether here on earth, on a spaceship, or on an unknown planet, some alien life form plants a spore or an egg in a human. Sometimes the carrier realizes what's happening, but most of the time he is unaware that he is a walking tabloid headline—MAN PREGNANT WITH ALIEN BABY. The person becomes a walking time bomb that finally explodes at breakfast one morning. The carrier's stomach begins to hurt, and it makes strange noises. Of course, we in the audience know exactly what's happening, but the person on screen is too concerned with his bacon and eggs to see the truth. We start yelling at the TV—"Get out of there! Drop the French Toast sticks and run!" But the person on screen never listens, and eventually, he explodes. Slime covers everything, and some second-rate Muppet wannabe comes out of the guy's chest. Every time I see this happen, I curl up in a little ball and twitch every twenty seconds, thinking that something just touched me.

Read James 1:15

Fill in the blanks
James 1:15 says, "Then, after _____ has conceived, it gives _____ to _____; and _____, when it is full-grown, gives birth to _____."

Lust is like an alien baby. It may be exciting at first, but when it explodes, it makes a mess of our lives. James tells us that if lustful desires go unchecked, they will give birth to sin and ultimately to death.

We see how this happens in the story of David. Yesterday, we saw how David's desires led him to have an affair with Bathsheba. He then sent her away, thinking no one would ever know—until she turned up pregnant. David's sin was about to become public knowledge, so he embarked on a scheme to trick Bathsheba's husband, Uriah. When David couldn't persuade Uriah to leave his battalion and go home and sleep with his wife, he planned Uriah's murder. As part of God's judgment, the child of the affair also died.

David's other children later battled lust and sexual sins, probably because of what they saw from their father. Lust conceived sin, and sin then gave birth to death.

■ **How did desire give birth to sin in David's story?**

_____

_____

_____

_____

■ **How did sin give birth to death in David's story?**

_____

_____

_____

_____

_____

God has created us to love and to be loved. This desire for love is good, and it's in all of us. But we are also broken people living in a broken world. Most of us—if not all of us—have been affected in some way by sexual sin, and we need to hear James' warning here. It's easy to draw imaginary lines with lust and think that we're OK as long as we don't cross those lines. But the point of avoiding lust is not to avoid pregnancy or sexually transmitted diseases. Too many know what it's like to have pornographic images trapped in their minds, to have sexual encounters they just can't forget, or to be unable to control their thoughts about someone else. These too are part of the destruction and death that lust causes.

God brings life from death, and his forgiveness covers all, but James reminds us that sin has consequences. Think about David—God forgave him but did not excuse him from the consequences of his decisions and actions.

Ask God to help you see the difference between a desire for love and a desire to lust. If this is a struggle for you, ask God to bring someone to mind who could help you walk through this battle with you. Thank God that he created you for so much more than lust.

another
path

   The longer I walk with Jesus as my friend and Savior, the more I realize that the one thing he truly desires of me is intimacy. Religion has in many ways distorted what our Father desires in his relationships with his people.

   Lust is one of the things that hinders a close connection with the Lord. It's not that God hates us or desires the worst for us because of our lust, but it does affect how we can relate to him. Scripture speaks repeatedly about the connection between a pure heart and seeing God for who he really is. Lust damages our hearts and thus our intimate connection with him.

   Think about this in the context of a marriage relationship. If one person is struggling with lust, it affects the love between the two. This does not mean that one spouse hates the other, but the lust must be dealt with if an intimate connection is going to happen. I love hearing stories of reconciliation and redemption in marriages, because they remind me of the reconciliation and redemption available from God.

■ **Do you struggle with any form of lust in your life?**

   ❏ yes
   ❏ no

If so, how does it affect your intimate connection with the Lord?

_____

_____

_____

_____

_____

■ Is Jesus serious about gouging your eye out if you lust? What is he trying to say here?

_____

_____

_____

_____

This shocking passage is a part of the Sermon on the Mount, and you can't read it without wondering how in the world you can live up to this. Every person on planet earth has lusted in his or her heart. Does that mean we should all gouge out our eyes?

What Jesus is doing here is showing us our desperate need for him. He is planting seeds in our hearts that show us how badly we need him to deliver us from the things that seem to control us and wreck our lives. The great thing about our Savior is that he doesn't just desire intimacy with us; he also gives us power in our weakness. He is not content for us to stay in our lust. He calls us to a life without this vice in our lives. Freedom and victory in this battle are possible. Could it be that so many people struggle with lust because they simply don't recognize and **accept** the amazing love God offers? We too often fall into a never-ending cycle of failing to accept God's love and thus falling deeper and deeper into the bondage of serving ourselves. But God offers another way; the way of love that Christ himself shows us.

There are other factors that point us toward lust. If we repeatedly put ourselves in positions where lust can take hold, we shouldn't be surprised when we fall. But eliminating the availability of lust will not answer the longings of our heart that lust reveals. Only an intimate connection with the true love of our heavenly Father can do that.

Most people preach against lust simply by saying "Stop it." We've all heard the do-better talks that do nothing to stop our behavior. Freedom from the bondage of lust comes from a much deeper source. Lust is largely an issue of intimacy with the creator of the world. The longing to lust is at its core a longing for a connection with God himself. Encountering the compassion and tenderness that he offers is an important step toward leaving the false intimacy of lust. Spend some time today sitting before Jesus and asking him to show you what it means to walk in true love with him.

VICE VERSA: FROM LUST TO LOVE

let's
talk about sex

■ Which of these descriptions do you think best reflects what God thinks about sex?

❑ Sex is good.
❑ Sex is bad.
❑ God doesn't care about sex and is not sure why he made it in the first place.
❑ Sex can be both good and bad.

Have you ever noticed how some things can be both good and bad at the same time? Take steak knives, for example. When I go to a steak house, I can pretty much tell how good the steak I ordered will be by the quality of steak knife I get. It's not a foolproof signal, but a big steak requires a big knife, so the knife can be a good sign. But if you try to take that same steak knife on board an airplane with you, you'll send the airport screeners into such a frenzy that the whole airport may shut down. I can barely get through the screening process now without feeling physically violated. I can't imagine what it would be like if I had a knife in my carry-on.

Cars are another example of this. They make our lives so much more convenient. When you have a car, a driver's license, and some gas money, you can go just about anywhere you want. But that same vehicle can also become a weapon or a coffin when used by a drunk driver or someone who insists on driving too fast. The thing that has the potential to be incredibly good also has the potential to be incredibly bad.

The same is true with sex. God is for sex. He created it. It is his idea. But sex used in the wrong way for the wrong purposes can be harmful to everyone involved.

Read 1 Corinthians 6:12-20
and 7:3-5

■ What is Paul's attitude toward sex in these verses?

❑ Paul hates sex and is mad at people for having it.
❑ Paul thinks sex is something that is no big deal.
❑ Paul thinks life is all about sex.
❑ None of the above

Fill in the blanks

First Corinthians 6:19-20 says, "Do you not _____ that your _____ is a _____ of the _____ _____, who is in you, whom you have _____ from God? You are not your _____; you were bought at a _____. Therefore _____ God with your _____."

Most of the time, when Christians address the topic of sex, they make one of two mistakes. They either think that sex is bad, God is against it, and we should abstain from it; or they think that sex is no big deal. Throughout church history and in our society today, we see these extremes. Some Christians in history were so against sex that they forbade it inside of marriage and even covered up the legs on their tables so as not to cause anyone to lust. (Personally, I don't see what covering up the legs on a table has to do with lust, but maybe that's just me.) Others have taken a lackadaisical attitude toward sex and acted as though God sets no restriction on it. But Paul shows us another way.

Paul shows us that God is for sex. He shows us that God is for lots of sex. Paul said that a husband and wife should have sex whenever either of them wants to do so. But Paul also cautioned the Corinthians against sexual immorality, which was way more prevalent in their society than it is even in our lust-filled world. He said that sex should take place between a man and a woman in a covenant marriage relationship and that, outside of such a relationship, sex is harmful instead of helpful.

Why did Paul make a distinction like this? Why would God create something that could be so good and so bad at the same time? Why would God guard against us entering into sex so casually yet be such a cheerleader for it in the right relationship? I think it's because God knows the power of acceptance and rejection on the human soul. God is not for abstinence, as is so often preached today. He is for sex inside of marriage. The reason is that God wants to create an environment where we will be most accepted where we are most truly known. Sex is a deeply intimate activity, and God wants to make sure that when we are this intimate, we will never be rejected.

Marriage is the covenant between a man and woman that says, "I accept you, and I will be with you no matter what." In the days of the Bible, when people made a covenant, they cut animals in two, walked between the halves and made a promise to each other signifying that what had been done to the animals should be done to them if they went back on their word. We keep some of this symbolism in weddings today, as the bride walks down the center aisle between family and friends.

While our society may no longer sense the depth of the covenant that marriage truly is, and divorce is an easy option for many, God wants us to experience a relationship where we are both fully known and fully accepted without any fear of rejection. This is something you can never get from a boyfriend or girlfriend. It is why rejection by someone with whom you have had sex hurts so bad and why sex in the proper marriage relationship can be so good. Marriage is intended to be a picture of our relationship with Christ—fully known, fully loved, fully accepted. Why would we settle for anything less?

prayer exercise:

Every time that sex comes to your mind today, pray that God would form within you a proper perspective and attitude toward sex. In the world we live in, sex is thrust upon us around every corner. Today, ask God to help you think about sex correctly by thinking about marriage every time something sexual comes to your mind. Use this exercise not just today but everyday as you live in a sexually charged world.

the right time

When you're a child, Christmas is the most romantic time of the year. It's a season full of beauty and mystery. When I was growing up, I loved the agonizing anticipation of it all—decorations, cold weather, breaks from school, family gatherings, special food, and movies like *A Christmas Story* and *It's a Wonderful Life*. As great as all these things were, they pointed toward the ultimate moment of the season—Christmas morning. When that time finally came, I went buck wild. I was euphoric ripping open the presents, and as soon as I'd finished I'd start looking forward to next Christmas morning.

■ What is the best Christmas present you ever received? Why was it the best?

_____

_____

_____

_____

Read Song of Solomon 8:1-4

Song of Solomon is a book that almost didn't make it into the Bible because it is so steamy. This book is basically two lovers writing back and forth about how they can't wait to get married, have sex, and love each other for the rest of their lives. They are very anxious to physically express the love they feel, but yet they wait.

■ On a scale from one to ten, how important is falling in love and getting married to you?

1 ←—————————— 5 ——————————→ 10

Fill in the blanks

Song on Solomon 8:4 says, "Daughters of Jerusalem, I charge you: Do not _____ or _____ _____ until it so _____."

■ What do you think this verse means?

_____

_____

_____

_____

■ What tempts you to arouse love (both emotionally and physically) before its time?

_____

_____

_____

_____

We don't usually think about it this way, but God created sex, and that means he knows how it works best. When God instructs us to put off lust and wait for sex, it's not because he's an old fuddy-duddy; it's because he knows sex is better in the context of marriage. This is the same principle that makes Christmas so much fun if we wait. When we guard the mystery and beauty until an agreed-upon time, it enhances the pleasure instead of diminishing it through vulgar familiarity.

I realized this the hard way the year I ruined Christmas. My brother and I were left home by ourselves one fateful December 9. We knew our parents had already been shopping, so we snooped all over the house until we discovered the hidden stash of toys and presents. My brother and I shouted and cheered as we feasted our eyes on our unwrapped presents. I even went so far as to take one game out of the box and start playing it.

My parents never found out what I did, but that was still the worst

Christmas I ever had. On Christmas morning, I had to fake excitement as I opened my presents. As I ripped open each present while trying to hide my guilt and regret, I realized that I had spoiled the beauty and mystery of Christmas by being impatient. This is the danger of lust and sexual sin—trading the momentary thrill of the wrong time for the lasting freedom of love inside a marriage relationship.

■ What are some ways you can guard the mystery and beauty of sex until the appropriate time?

_____

_____

_____

_____

■ How will doing this give you the freedom to love your future spouse?

_____

_____

_____

prayer exercise:

Take some time to pray for your future spouse and your marriage. Pray that God will help you not to awaken love until the appropriate time. Thank God for the gift of sex and ask him to protect you from lust so that you can have the freedom to love at the right time.

_____

_____

_____

_____

_____

_____

_____

_____

_____

_____

_____

_____

_____

   This page is designed to give you space to take notes during your "Vice Versa" group session or to journal your reflections on the highlights of this week's study.

WEEK THREE

from sloth to passion
(waking up from the numbness)

Novocain
and following God

We continue our study of *Vice Versa* this week by looking at the sin of sloth. I know the word sloth may seem a little old-fashioned to you—if you even know what it means—but if you will bear with us this week, you may discover that no vice that we mention in this book impacts you more than this one. When ancient people talked about sloth, they were talking about both laziness and numbness. It's the sense of being alive but letting life pass you by. It's an absence of passion.

Read Luke 7:36-50

■ What was the difference between the Pharisee and the woman in this passage?

_____

_____

_____

■ Who really acted as the host in this passage?

❑ the Pharisee
❑ the woman

Explain your answer.

_____

_____

_____

I hate going to the dentist. I always have. Now, one of my good friends is my dentist, but it doesn't make going any more tolerable. You sit there with your head tilted back in an awkward position trying not to swallow as they put what tastes like sand on your teeth. I never realized how often I swallowed until I was told not to. The hygienist pokes your gums with sharp metal objects that seem like torture devices, not dental tools, and then flosses your teeth so violently that it produces enough blood for your appointment to be rated R. I'm convinced that the hygienist doesn't think that she's done her job until she sees you bleed.

But even the worst cleaning I've had is better than the best filling. The shots that numb your mouth with Novocain so that you won't feel the drilling are the best part of the experience—and that's not saying much. For what feels like hours, the dentist drills away at your teeth in a manner that would make a carpenter proud. The sounds and the force are traumatic, and on top of that you leave unable to feel one side of your mouth. For hours, tingles and numbness mask the pain you should be feeling, and for that you are thankful.

The funny part comes when you try to eat. Your taste buds are numb, so everything tastes bland like lima beans. Plus, the Novocain makes your mouth so numb that it's almost impossible to keep food in your mouth without drooling. Your lips are like speed bumps—oversized and only good for slowing things down, not for stopping anything from going over them. So you make a fool of yourself, dropping food all over your shirt without even knowing it.

I bring up this experience because I think it's the way a lot of us go through life. Numbness is a reality for many of us. Just as numbness from Novocain not only dulls the pain but also makes it impossible for us to taste food, spiritual numbness keeps us from experiencing God. Many of us have become numb because of pain we have experienced or pain that threatens us, while others of us are numb because life has become so routine and monotonous. But all of us need to recognize that numbness is a spiritual problem in our lives.

In this passage, the Pharisee was around Jesus but missed him. He let life pass him by. On the other hand, the woman, who knew who she was and also who Jesus was, threw herself at Jesus' feet, poured perfume on them, kissed them, and wiped them with her hair. The Pharisee is a picture of numbness, and the woman is a picture of passion.

The question for us this week is which of these pictures best describes our relationship with Jesus. Are we just around Jesus, content to have him in our house? Or are our lives poured out at his feet with the kind of passion that makes life worth living?

- How would you describe passion?

_____

_____

_____

- When is the last time that you can honestly say you were passionate about God?

_____

_____

_____

prayer exercise:

Take some perfume or cologne and put it on your pillow. This week let the fragrance remind you as you go to sleep of the journey from sloth to passion on which God calls us to embark. Pray as you go to sleep tonight and each night that God will kindle passion for Him in your life.

feeling
the pain

■ List three scars you have and briefly describe how you got them. Put a check next to the examples where someone such as a parent, friend, or doctor had to help you.

_____

_____

_____

_____

_____

_____

Every scar has a story. I have huge semicircle scar that runs the length of my thumb. Here's the story behind the scar.

I grew up watching action movies. I was desperate to craft myself into a mean, lean, fighting machine, and I quickly learned that if you want to be tough, you have to ignore the pain. I watched the movie *Predator* and was mesmerized as a team of commandos marched through a tropical forest wearing sleeveless shirts that showed off their bulging muscles and hunted down an elusive enemy. In one scene, a soldier tells Blain that he is bleeding, and Blain responds, "I ain't got time to bleed." For a seventh-grade boy, seeing that was a milestone moment in my life, on par with getting my first Nintendo system.

Unfortunately, when I cut my hand open with a kitchen knife two days later, I had plenty of time both to bleed and to run through the house calling for my mommy. The truth is that, although I wasn't being all that tough, it would have been silly for me to act as if this wound didn't hurt. It would have been dumb to cover up the gash and not tell anyone I was hurting.

Instead of having a scar from the 11 stitches I got, I would have a disfigured and maybe even permanently damaged thumb.

So why, when it comes to the emotional scars in our lives, do we try to hide the pain from others and even from ourselves? Do we think if we whisper, "I don't have time to bleed," the pain will just go away?

- Do you find it easy to tell God about the things that have hurt you?
    - ❑ yes
    - ❑ no

- When you struggle with sin, is it easier for you to pretend that it doesn't affect you than to ask for help?
    - ❑ yes
    - ❑ no

- List three things that have scarred you emotionally things that were tough for you to deal with either when they happened, after the fact, or both.

_____

_____

_____

_____

_____

Jeremiah was a famous prophet. He could even be considered a religious action hero for all the things he went through. He fought on the front lines on God's behalf, but things did not go well for him. Let's see how this prophet responded to the pain he felt.

■ Have you ever heard someone pray with this much honesty before?

❏ yes
❏ no

Why do you think Jeremiah prayed this way?

_____

_____

The first step in moving from sloth to passion, from being numb to having purpose, is to feel and process the pain in our lives, as Jeremiah did. When we are not honest with God about what we feel and how we feel, we run the danger of growing spiritually numb, while thinking we're exhibiting politeness and respect. If you visit an addiction support group such as Alcoholics Anonymous, almost every person there will tell you he abused a drug because he couldn't deal with the pain in his life. These addicts drink or smoke or shoot up so that they won't feel themselves bleeding emotionally.

We are all wounded in our own ways. But that doesn't mean we have to be numb. Wounded people don't have to go to church looking for a fake smile and false assurances that everything will be OK. They can look for someone to bleed with them and to remind them that passion is possible, even in the midst of pain.

prayer exercise:

Acknowledging the pain in our lives is a vital step in moving from sloth to passion. We call prayers like the one Jeremiah prayed here laments, and the fact that they're in the Bible shows us that it's OK to approach God in this way. Write an honest letter to God that honestly expresses the pain and passion in your life. After you write it, read back through it, remembering that our greatest pain often helps us see what our greatest passions are. Ask God to be with you in your pain and to begin to reveal your passions to you.

_____

_____

_____

_____

_____

from pain
to passion

Pain comes in all different shapes and sizes. Although it is something we usually try to avoid, the truth is that it's all around us. So if, as we saw in Day Two, becoming numb isn't the answer to pain, then what is?

This past Christmas, I went shopping at the mall with my wife and daughter. I'm not a big shopper, but my wife is, and every Christmas she combs the malls looking for deals and just the right gifts for our friends and family. Every once in a while, she drags me along to be a part of the process. I'd love to tell you that I get excited about these trips, but I don't. Most of the time, I'm dazed and confused and suffering from something I call "mall leg." I can walk to play 18 holes of golf or run up and down the basketball court without a problem, but if I spend 15 minutes walking around the mall, my legs are shot.

The reason I bring all this up is that every Christmas we walk around the mall trying to find presents that the people in our lives need. This is no easy task. We've all had Christmases where we opened presents like socks or underwear only to become bold-faced liars by acting as though these gifts were just what we wanted or needed. So when we shop, we try hard to find gifts that will meet a need.

The test of a good Christmas present is whether it is used three months after Christmas. Sometimes, it turns out we didn't really want the things we thought we did. And sometimes, the presents we weren't excited about at the time become the most useful. At the last White Elephant Christmas party I attended, I spent the whole party trying to get back the Outback Steakhouse gift certificate I had brought, but in the end I was just one more set of hands that certificate went through. I was left with a shaving kit—much like the one that was already sitting on my bathroom counter. But the thing is, this shaving kit has become one of the presents I have used the most. The latch on my old kit suddenly broke, and I was glad another one had come my way. Instead of having to pay for a new kit, I turned to the gift I didn't know I would need.

Pain is something few seek out, but often it turns out to be a gift we didn't know we needed, because out of pain grows passion. Passion can develop in other places, such as deep conviction of a certain truth or a great love for something that we value. But in pain, we are reminded that we are needy, and this sense of need is one of the most powerful places for passion to be born.

Read John 21:1-19

- What pain was Peter experiencing in this passage?

_____

_____

_____

- What needs did that pain reveal?

_____

_____

_____

We see Peter in great pain here. You might not see it in this particular passage, but the chapter before tells us how Peter claimed he would follow Jesus to the death—only to abandon him when the going got tough. On the night when Jesus was beaten and tried, Peter denied him, only to realize later what he had done and flee weeping. After Jesus rose from the dead, Peter felt more like an outsider and a traitor to the faith than a disciple.

This passage shows how Jesus restored Peter, showing grace and mercy while recalling him to follow. Jesus met Peter in the midst of his pain and need and redeemed all of it. Peter probably never got over this moment. And while Peter had shown excitement and hints of passion before, the pain of denial and the joy of restoration set him free for the rest of his life. He still made some mistakes, as Acts tells us, but he would not be numb. Peter became a passionate pursuer of Christ.

Take some time to meditate on the following questions: Will you give the pain in your life to Christ today? Will you sense your need for Christ through your pain? Will you trust that the pain you feel today will fuel your passion tomorrow? Will you begin to run free?

passion
unleashed

Acts
2:1-41

Pain is not the only breeding ground for passion, but it is one of the most powerful. Still, you can be passionate about something that has never brought you pain. Love, conviction, and past experiences are also sources of passion. For example, my passion for soccer comes out of my love of playing. My passion for my wife and daughter comes from a love relationship with them. My passion for TNT hot wings comes out of my deep conviction that there is no better wings restaurant on the planet. To this day, whenever someone comes to visit me for the first time, I make sure they experience some TNT wings, and I'm not satisfied until they agree that these are the greatest wings they've ever had.

No matter the source of passion, it's interesting to see how passion grows as it is put into practice. As a fire needs to be fanned to grow, passion must be put into action, or it will turn into mere good intentions and then drift into numbness. Laziness and numbness are cousins. While busyness is no guarantee of passion, it is clear that passion is never content to stay on the sidelines.

Read Acts 2:1-41

■ What happened to the disciples in this passage?

❑ They were called to action by a great motivational speaker.

❑ They experienced the Holy Spirit.

■ What did the disciples do as a result of this experience?

_____

_____

_____

```
Fill in the blanks
In Acts 2:32 33, Peter said, "God has
raised this _____ to life, and we
are all _____ of the fact.
Exalted to the right hand of _____,
he has _____ from the _____
the promised _____ _____ and
has _____ out what you now _____
and _____."
```

Maybe the reason so many of us struggle to unleash passion in our lives is that we are not experiencing God. We may know a lot about God, and we may even carry out some disciplines of faith such as reading the Bible or praying. But really experiencing God and the power of living by the Spirit is just not something in which many of us are interested. We want a set of beliefs that we can check off. We want a way to get to heaven. We may even be OK with a set of rules of right and wrong. But in all this, we never really know the God that this whole "following God thing" is about. We don't have passion because God is a stranger, a distant father we appeal to only when times are tough.

In this passage, the same Peter we talked about in Day Three addressed the crowd. He was no longer the coward we see at the end of the gospels; he was now a confident man of faith and the rock that would lead the church. His message dripped with passion. He was not on the sidelines anymore. He had experienced restoration from his pain and the power of the Spirit. He could be silent no longer. He would not be content until the world knew what (and whom) he knew.

Reflect on these words from Revelation 3:14-16: "To the angel of the church in Laodicea write: 'These are the words of the Amen, the faithful and true witness, the ruler of God's creation. I know your deeds, that you are neither cold nor hot. I wish you were either one or the other! So, because you are lukewarm—neither hot nor cold—I am about to spit you out of my mouth."

Numbness breaks the heart of God, and it is no good for us, either. The choice to be passionate is the choice to join God in life instead of merely sitting on the sidelines and letting God and life pass you by. It may involve waiting for a time, but once you realize your neediness and experience God's grace, you cannot ride the pine.

- What are you afraid of? What is keeping you from joining the game spiritually?

_____

_____

_____

_____

Release these things to the Father now. He knows your fears and questions. Seek after him. Desire him. Long for him. Today, take the opportunity to fast for one meal. Every time you get hungry, use that longing to remind you to long for God. Every time the thought of food comes to your mind, cry out to him. Seek him with your whole heart. Do not be satisfied to stay on the sidelines. Join the experience of passion.

VICE VERSA: FROM SLOTH TO PASSION

Luke
4:14-21

freedom
to move

After spending a week journeying from sloth to passion, you may be asking questions like these: "What now? I am experiencing God; I long for and desire him; but how does that affect the way I work or go to school? How does this affect my future dreams and plans?" Today, we're going to take the time to funnel and refine the passion we've been stirring up all week.

Read Luke 4:14-21

- Put verses 18-19 in your own words in eight words or less.

_____

_____

This passage of Scripture shows us the heart of Jesus' ministry. He brought healing to people and places that were broken spiritually, emotionally, physically, socially, and in any other way we can imagine. This is the same ministry that was carried on by the disciples and that has been passed on to us. The Christian call is to make beauty out of ashes and to put back together things that are broken with the vision of Christ and by the power of the Spirit. Each of us plays a role in this process. Our world is filled with brokenness, and God has gifted each of us with talents, skills, and abilities. Living by faith means giving our hands the opportunity to make a difference in the brokenness that our eyes see.

- Where around you right now can you see brokenness?

_____

_____

_____

Following God — Vice Versa 61

- What talents, gifts, and abilities has God given you?

_____

_____

_____

_____

- How can you use your talents, gifts, and abilities to impact the brokenness you listed?

_____

_____

_____

_____

By answering these questions, you are well on the way to living with passion. Now the biggest challenge before you is having the faith to get off the sidelines and into life. Sloth lets life pass you by. But life doesn't have to be that way. You can live with passion, jumping into life with both feet and trusting the Spirit of God to guide your eyes and hands as you bring forth the kingdom of God by birthing beauty out of brokenness.

prayer exercise:

Pray that God would give you the courage to put into practice the things that you have discovered this week. Reflect on the word Immanuel, a name for Jesus that means "God with us."

_____

_____

_____

_____

_____

_____

_____

_____

_____

_____

_____

_____

_____

_____

_____

_____

This page is designed to give you space to take notes during your "Vice Versa" group session or to journal your reflections on the highlights of this week's study.

WEEK FOUR

from envy to blessing
(breaking free from the competition game)

Mine!
the perils of envy

I have discovered a disease that is highly contagious among females. I'm not sure why it is, but every time I ask my wife what she wants as we order at a drive-through window, she gets the wrong thing. How do I know this? Because halfway through my meal, she starts asking me for some of my food. For instance, I may ask if she wants french fries with the burger she ordered, and she says no. I order fries with my meal because I want them. But as we drive away, I see my wife chowing down on my fries. Even worse, when I start to eat my meal, it always feels as though I'm eating under a watchful eye. My wife stares at whatever I've ordered, no matter what it is, and gives me big puppy-dog eyes that beg me to give up my food and trade it for what she has.

I used to think I was alone in this predicament, but then I began to notice how often my buddies' wives do the same thing. Every time, the guy acts the same way. Frustrated by his wife's actions, he pulls his food close to his chest and surrounds it with his arms. It's a savage motion, really, like he just made a kill and will share what he conquered with no one. I hate to admit it, but some of the biggest fights my wife and I have had were over french fries. She tries to sneak past my arms to get the fries she wanted but didn't order—probably because she thinks if she eats my fries, the calories don't count like they would if they were hers. Meanwhile, I'm pulling a *Karate Kid* wax-on, wax-off move to ward her off. She gets frustrated, and then I get frustrated. Before I know it, I find myself in the doghouse.

Now that I know how the routine works, I stop her in mid-sentence at the drive-through and order fries for her. She sometimes thinks the extra 99 cents will break the budget, but I consider that a cost well worth paying so that I can live to fight another day.

Read Numbers 12

Envy is the attitude that says, "I want what you have, and I don't want you to have what I have." It's one of the deepest sicknesses of the human soul. We pick it up early in life, shouting "Mine!" as we fight over toys, and it never really changes. The life of envy is life on the treadmill, focused on making sure you have more than everyone around you and that they all know it.

In this passage, Miriam and Aaron succumbed to this disease. Moses was the leader of Israel, and his siblings Miriam and Aaron didn't like the woman he had married. At least, that was the excuse they used as they tried to push Moses out of leadership. But things didn't work out well for them. Miriam came down with a case of leprosy, and Aaron feared for his life as well and pleaded for Moses to intercede with God on their behalf. Moses did so and in the process showed why he was the true leader of Israel in the first place.

If we are not careful, envy will take hold in our lives just as it did with Miriam and Aaron. Much of our society today is based on the idea of envy. We want to have what everyone else has, and then we want to be the only one who has it. Just walk into a dance where two girls are wearing the same dress and see each claim that the other is wearing "my dress." Or listen to the whispers of the backup quarterback as he swears that he could do much better than the starter. Envy is everywhere, and if we are not careful, it will take over our lives.

■ **How do you struggle with envy in your life?**

_____

_____

_____

_____

■ **When was the last time you wanted what someone else had so much that it dominated your thoughts? Explain that situation.**

_____

_____

_____

_____

- How did you deal with envy in your life?
  - ❏ I got what I wanted.
  - ❏ I took what I wanted from the person who had it.
  - ❏ Once I got what I wanted, I looked down on others who didn't have it.
  - ❏ I didn't get what I wanted, and I got angry about it.
  - ❏ Other _____

We're going to seek to move this week away from the vice of envy toward the life of freedom that comes from being a person of contentment and blessing. The struggle will be hard, but it's worth it. Aren't you tired of always being in competition with others? Aren't you exhausted from trying to keep up with the Joneses? Maybe it's because we were never meant to live that way.

prayer exercise:

List the top ten things you want right now and then explain why you want those things. Be honest and indicate how many of these things you want just because someone else has them. Ask God to help you break free of envy this week and to help you imagine another way to live.

_____

_____

_____

_____

stop
climbing

Tryouts for the football team were more than three months away, but I couldn't wait to start working out. I dreamed of being the best football player in the history of my school. I stared at the ceiling every night, imagining making the big catch that would send our team to the state championship game. I spent most of my free time in the front yard throwing the football with my dad and my brother. I ran, lifted weights, and did stretching exercises. I even changed what I ate so that I would get stronger and fitter. I constantly thought about what I could do to make myself a better football player, and I was willing to do whatever it took to be the best.

Like every young football player, I dreamed of being great. I watched football on TV and wondered what it would be like to be a star. I wanted to be famous. Unfortunately, as it turned out I was too short, too weak, and too slow.

We don't mind dreaming big, even though it sometimes seems ridiculous. The truth is, we're willing to do whatever it takes to climb the ladder and be the best. But there's one problem. Not only do we want to be the best; we secretly want the worst for the people we are competing against for the dream job or starring role we covet. We want them to fail so that we can succeed. That's how I felt when I went out for the football team. I don't want to admit it, but I was extremely selfish and insecure as I pursued my goals. In my mind, it was all about me.

■ **Why do you think we are driven to be the best at what we do?**

_____

_____

_____

_____

Read Mark 9:33-37

■ How do you define greatness?

_____

_____

_____

■ How is Jesus' view of greatness different than ours?

_____

_____

_____

Fill in the blanks
In Mark 9:35, Jesus says, "If anyone wants to be _____, he must be the very _____, and the _____ of _____."

Jesus is not against us seeking to be the best at what we do—not at all. But he does not want us to do so at the expense of other people. When we think of greatness this way, we miss the point. In this passage, Jesus gives us a different picture of greatness by saying that the first will be last and the last will be first. It's more important to **do our best** than **to be the best.** Greatness in the kingdom of God comes from taking the last seat and serving others.

The disciples in this passage were concerned about the wrong thing. They thought greatness came from climbing the ladder, and they were willing to step all over each other to get there. All they were doing was thinking about themselves. Greatness isn't a problem, but the way we often define it is. We don't have a problem with God's blessing as long as we're the ones being blessed. But if someone else receives the blessing instead of us, we get competitive and try to take his place. That's what the disciples were doing here.

But Jesus confronted their envy and competition and called them to a different kind of greatness.

Jesus calls us to a different way of life, one that turns the other cheek and wishes great blessings for other people. Greatness doesn't come from climbing over people; it comes from serving them.

prayer exercise:

Spend some time asking the Holy Spirit to show you what it means to be great in the Father's eyes. Confess to the Lord that you want to become a person that desires blessings for other people, not just for yourself. Enjoy his presence in a moment of quiet.

first
steps

When I was 4, the nursery school I attended had a pet hamster. I don't remember the hamster's name, but he looked like every other hamster I've ever seen. I spent part of each day at school looking at the hamster and thinking about its life. Honestly, it seemed downright boring to me. He lived in a little cage and pretty much just ate and slept. The highlight of his day came when he climbed into his little hamster wheel and began running, causing the wheel to spin faster and faster. Before long, though, the hamster would get tired, stop running, and return to his favorite napping spot.

The life of envy is a lot like being on the hamster wheel. You constantly run, but you end up in the same exact place, tired and exhausted and burned out from trying to keep up with the other hamsters that appear to be running faster. And while a little running is good for everyone, living on the wheel does us no good. The vice of envy traps us by keeping us on the wheel—never satisfied, never having enough, always looking to what everyone else has and trying to take these things from others at any expense.

Read Philippians 4:10-13

Fill in the blanks
Philippians 4:11 says, "I am not _____ this because I am in _____, for I have _____ to be _____ whatever the _____."

■ Who is the most contented person you know?

_____

Why is that person content?

_____

_____

■ How did that person learn to be content?

_____

_____

_____

_____

Verse 13 in this passage may be one of the most misused in all of Scripture. We often hear it quoted by someone who wants to win a game, pass a test or accomplish something great. But when the verse is used this way, it is taken out of context, and we miss its true meaning. It's pretty ironic that this verse, which is about contentment, is so often used to encourage us to get on the hamster wheel instead of leading us to get off it. Paul isn't talking about winning here. The "do" refers more to enduring something than conquering it. It's about finding peace in whatever life deals you (win or lose), not about assuring a victory every time.

The first step in breaking free from envy is learning the secret of contentment. Envy leads me to want what you have and for you not to have it at all. But contentment leads me to be OK with having what I have and with you having what you have. Learning to be content means accepting that there will always be someone who has more than you and finding a way to live with that. This is the secret to breaking free from the hamster wheel and avoiding spending your life chasing unnecessary things. This leads to the peace of being OK with yourself that comes from trusting the grace of God in life's mountains and valleys.

Paul knew this peace. That's why, in the middle of thanking the Philippian church for the help it had sent him, he could say that he had learned to trust God no matter what he was going through. He had eaten well when things were good and thanked God for it. He had eaten little when things were tough and trusted God in those times too. He had learned to be satisfied in whatever state of life God placed him.

We can learn a lot from Paul's words in this passage. In a world that pushes us onto the hamster wheel, we must learn what to value. We will never find satisfaction if we seek it in the ways the world does. A Christian's satisfaction comes not from life's circumstances but from the God who walks through all of life's circumstances with her. Contentment is the first step toward embracing freedom from envy. We'll see over the next two days how we can take more steps and walk and jump and fly freely.

Take a moment to chart your life using the diagram below. What have been the high points? What have been the low points? Once you have filled in some of these episodes from your life, go back and circle the ones in which you can honestly say you were content and satisfied. You may find that you were more content in the hard times than in the good ones because you leaned more heavily in those times on the arms of the Father or less content in the good times because you wanted even more. Use what you learn about yourself during this exercise to guide your prayer time as you identify where you are right now on the chart and thank and trust God in this time of your life.

unlikely
blessings

Read Matthew 5:3-11

■ From this list of people Jesus described as blessed, which three are most like you?

_____

_____

_____

_____

■ Which three are least like you?

_____

_____

_____

_____

■ Name someone whom you consider a hero.

_____

Which of the qualities that Jesus names here does that person have?

_____

_____

Picture sitting with a group of your friends at your favorite pizza place. After everyone has ordered, you clear your throat to get everyone's attention and confidently declare, "I am pleased to announce that we are all blessed. We will now spend long hours training so that we can run toward danger instead of away from it. We will smash down doors and climb ladders hundreds of feet into the air to break through windows. We will do all of this in excruciating temperatures while wearing hundreds of pounds of equipment. Some of us will die doing this, and none of us will get rich. Who's with me?"

Chances are you would only see for a moment that no one raised their hands before someone threw a piece of pepperoni pizza in your face. Your friends would think you were crazy to say something like that. But this is exactly what the men and women of any local fire department choose to do when they become firefighters, and it's exactly what many in the Fire Department of New York (FDNY) had to do on September 11, 2001. This is the calling of heroes.

This scenario is what it must have been like for those who heard Jesus tell them they were blessed because of poverty, meekness, and mercy. This is an even more unlikely path of blessing than becoming a firefighter. But Jesus taught that, no matter what situation we are in, we are to bring blessing and change to the world. This path of blessing—a path that turns us into heroes as we travel down it—is a hard one, but God in his grace gives us the power to walk it.

Jesus speaks in this passage in a manner called **unconditional performative language.** Basically, that's a fancy way of saying that Jesus isn't describing something that already is; he is making these descriptions a reality as he declares them. In other words, Jesus isn't just describing what a hero of his kingdom looks like; he is making us heroes through his words! We don't become blessings because we are perfect; we become blessings because Jesus sees things in us that we can't even see yet. Instead of living in envy and jealousy and competition, we can realize that we are blessed, and we can offer that blessing to others. Jesus calls us blessed heroes.

Reread Matthew 5:3-11. This time, insert your name in the verses. (For example, "Blessed is Chris, who hungers and thirsts after righteousness, for he will be filled.") As you read the verses this way, hear Jesus speaking the truth of blessing into your life. Thank him for blessing you and ask him to show you how you can be a blessing to others.

VICE VERSA: FROM ENVY TO BLESSING

tickets
and toys

A few weeks ago, I returned to a place I had not visited in quite a while. One of my friend's sons was celebrating a birthday, and the party was at Chuck E. Cheese. Kids love few things more than a place where they can eat pizza, play video games, and watch dancing rodents. Kids were running around everywhere, playing games and collecting tickets so that they could get the perfect toy from the display counter.

As I watched this, I thought back to when I was a kid and how much those tickets meant to me. I remember playing Skee-Ball, Pop-a-Shot, and other games, hoping to get a high score so that more tickets would shoot out of the dispenser. The more tickets I collected, the better the prize was at the end of the day.

Now that I'm an adult, I realize how cheap the toys in the display counter are. I know now it would be much cheaper just to buy the toys than to play the games over and over again to get enough tickets to "win" them. But even at my age, hearing the sounds of games and tickets sent chills down my spine.

I know that, as an adult, I'm not supposed to be as excited about these games as the kids are. So when my grown-up friends and I took over the game room, it was a little embarrassing. We tried to be as polite as possible, but part of me wanted to elbow the kids aside and prove in a Billy Madison moment that I still had what it took to rule Chuck E. Cheese. We crowded around the Skee-Ball lanes and the Pop-a-Shot machine to compete. Tickets flowed out of the machines, and since our kids were too young to appreciate the games, we used their tokens like six-year-olds who just won the lottery. You can probably imagine that the rivalry got intense. Like little kids begging their parents for more tokens, we went to our wives, asking if we could play just one more time and win some more tickets. (I think our wives pitied us, but they played along so as not to smash our fragile egos.)

As the party ended, we finally returned to our senses and remembered that we didn't really need the cool 5,000-ticket Spider-Man figure. So we decided to take all our tickets and give them to one kid who had barely been able to win any. This kid thought he had hit the jackpot. I'll never forget the look on his face. It was like someone had opened a bank vault and told him he could have everything inside. He nervously counted out all the tickets as his friends looked on in amazement. That day, I was amazed at the power that passing along a little grace could have in someone's life.

Read 1 Kings 17:7-24

■ What did Elijah ask of the widow?

_____

_____

■ How do you think the widow felt as she gave her flour and oil to Elijah?

❏ scared   ❏ angry   ❏ jealous
❏ anxious   ❏ excited   ❏ other_____

■ Would you have been willing to give what the widow did?

   ❏ yes
   ❏ no

■ How did the widow's life of blessing help Elijah?

_____

_____

_____

_____

■ How did the widow's life of blessing end up helping her?

_____

_____

_____

This week, we've described envy as my wanting what you have and not wanting you to have it at all. On Day 3, we saw that contentment is being OK with what I have and being OK with what you have. Blessing goes even further. It is wanting you to have what I have or wanting you to have what I don't have. Contentment is great, but the life of blessing is even better.

Christianity is not a movement of contentment; it is a movement of blessing. A Christian passes on grace and heals brokenness. A Christian gives of himself because Christ has given himself to us. The life of blessing allows us to break free of the competition game and travel in a different direction. It allows us to step off the hamster wheels and experience what life is really about—giving ourselves to others. And when we give ourselves away, we often discover that we gain more than we could ever give.

prayer exercise:

Take a walk outside and think about all the ways that God has blessed you. What grace has been given to you because of the sacrifice of others? Consider how you can be an agent of blessing in the lives of others. Ask God to help you to get off and stay off the hamster wheel of envy and start experiencing the life that seeks to give itself away.

_____

_____

_____

_____

_____

_____

_____

_____

_____

_____

_____

_____

_____

_____

This page is designed to give you space to take notes during your "Vice Versa" group session or to journal your reflections on the highlights of this week's study.

WEEK FIVE

from greed to sacrifice
(from all-in to all-out)

the poverty
of abundance

■ What are your five most valuable possessions?

_____

_____

_____

■ If you inherited a million dollars,
what five things would you buy?

_____

_____

_____

Read Luke 12:13-21

■ What (if anything) did the landowner
in this parable do wrong?

_____

_____

■ What should he have done with his big
harvest?

_____

_____

■ List again the things you would buy with a million dollars, but this time indicate whether they would benefit other people or just you.

_____

_____

_____

A televised interview with a man who lost his house and all his possessions to a raging brush fire driven by Santa Ana winds in California provides a sharp contrast to the landowner in this parable. This man had just seen everything he owned go up in smoke, but he recalled that his brother had recently told him that what we own winds up owning us, and so he enthusiastically told a reporter, "I am a free man now."

I'm not trying to say that, if we realize that greed has taken root in our hearts, we need to set all our possessions on fire. But we do need to see the danger of constantly trying to get more and more stuff. If you look honestly at your life, you'll realize that not much has changed from your toddler days, when you grabbed every toy you could get your hands on and yelled, "Mine!" We're obsessed with having the latest clothes, the coolest cars, and the best cell phones.

This parable is not a warning against having possessions; it is a warning about your possessions having you. It's so easy for us to slip into greed, especially when we think everyone around us has so much more than we do. But we can move from greed to sacrifice. I learned how to do this with the help of my dad and Aunt Jemima®. On Saturday mornings when I was growing up, my dad would make pancakes for my brother and me. He made big pancakes and an even bigger mess, and we loved it. I couldn't eat them fast enough. But not once did I take a pancake off my brother's plate and stuff it in my pocket to save for later. If dad put a huge pancake on my plate before I finished my first one, I had no problem giving it to my brother if he was ready for seconds, because I knew there was an endless supply from my father, who delighted in giving his children what they needed. How much more does God delight in providing for his children and in watching them share and sacrifice with one another!

- Look back at your lists of possessions and desired possessions. How can you keep these things from owning you?

_____

_____

_____

- How can you share these things with others?

_____

_____

_____

prayer exercise:

Ask God to point out places in your life where greed has taken hold, and ask him to give you eyes to see the needs of those around you and the courage to make a sacrifice to meet those needs.

money
or makeover

The word echoes during the opening credits of the hit reality show *The Apprentice*: money, money, money, money. Society tells us that money makes the world go round. In Week Four, we saw how we're told we need more and more. This is especially true when it comes to money. No matter what income bracket we are in, we always seem to need a little more to make ends meet.

We rarely take time to reflect on how our pursuit of money affects us and those around us. Let's be perfectly clear: Making money is not bad. Having money is not bad. In fact, God may bless some of us with the ability to make a lot of money. But when we stop being generous and start hoarding our money at the expense of those in need, we miss the freedom that Christ longs to bring to our lives.

Read Acts 5:1-11

■ What is your reaction to this story?

❑ shock   ❑ joy   ❑ hope
❑ conviction   ❑ anger   ❑ anxiety
❑ peace   ❑ questions
❑ other _____

■ Do you think God overreacted in this story?

❑ yes
❑ no

Explain your answer.

_____

_____

_____

This is a shocking story, to say the least. When I first read this passage, it seems to me like God overreacted. Why couldn't Ananias and Sapphira do whatever they wanted with their property? Shouldn't Peter and the church be thankful they decided to give anything at all? These questions are natural after reading this story.

But we have to observe this story in context to understand what is really taking place. As we will see in Day Three of this lesson, the early church embodied the heart of Christ by giving of themselves. People often sold property and gave the proceeds to the church to help those in need. And the needs were many—people were being persecuted, and their stuff was often seized. The church and its members stepped in and sacrificially took care of the poor and helpless.

Enter Ananias and Sapphira. They vowed to sell a piece of property and give the money to the church as others had. But once the property sold and they had the money in their hands, things changed. Maybe they got more for the property than they expected. Maybe they had some expenses come up in their own lives. Whatever the case, once the money was in their hands, they had a hard time letting go. So they decided to lie and tell the church elders that they had sold the property for less than they actually had, and they kept the difference for themselves. When each of them lied to the elders about what they had done, they were struck dead.

God's harshness in this story is striking. To be honest, it makes me anxious. I know I have lied in the past, and I'm sure I could be more generous in my offerings to the church. I feel sorry for Ananias and Sapphira in some ways, and I wonder why God was so hard on them but so merciful to me. I don't know the answers to these questions, but I do have some observations.

The book of Acts shows us how, with the movement of the Holy Spirit, the gospel spread like wildfire. As people gave of themselves, the message went all over the world. Despite persecution, the Roman Empire couldn't stop this explosion, and neither could the Jewish establishment. The only thing that could get in the gospel's way was the people's selfish ambition. Only if people stopped giving would the movement lose its impact.

Ananias and Sapphira's actions stood in stark contrast to the movement of the church. They started saying, "Mine," and nothing ends giving quicker than a few selfish people. In a world where giving was the norm, selfishness was a serious offense. Maybe God valued the spread of the gospel and the power of the Spirit so much that he wouldn't let anything get in the way. Maybe his act of judgment was really an act of mercy. Maybe, if Ananias and

Sapphira had lived, others would have started saying, "Mine," and the spread of the gospel would have slowed or even stopped.

We live in a very different world today. Giving is rare, and selfishness is normal. That means there is no better way for us to stand out than by being generous. The reason *Extreme Makeover: Home Edition* has become a hit show is that it gives us a picture of what the gospel community is supposed to look like. Freedom comes from realizing that our stuff comes from God and letting go by giving that stuff to others. Greed kills by shutting down the Spirit in our lives, and freedom is found not in financial security but in sacrifice.

prayer exercise:

Visit the *Extreme Makeover: Home Edition* website at abc.com/primetime/xtremehome/index.html.

Read the stories of generosity and selflessness there, and as you do, ask God to help you move from greed to sacrifice this week. Ask him to help you value what he values. As you pray, hold your hands open with your palms facing up as an act of letting go.

VICE VERSA: FROM GREED TO SACRIFICE

where's
the beef?

Read Acts 4:32-37

Fill in the blanks
Acts 4:32 says, "_____ the _____
were _____ in heart and mind. No one
_____ that _____ of his
_____ were his _____, but
they _____ everything they had."

■ How does the picture in these verses
contrast with the picture in yesterday's passage?

_____

_____

_____

■ Which picture best describes your
experience with church?

   ❏ Ananias and Sapphira
   ❏ Barnabas and the early church

■ What can you do to make sure that the
people you know experience what
church is intended to be?

_____

_____

_____

During the 1980s, a popular Wendy's commercial featured an elderly woman ordering a hamburger at a fast-food restaurant. When she got her order, the woman lifted up the bun to see lettuce, tomato, pickles, ketchup, and mustard but only a tiny burger patty. She complained by saying, "Where's the beef?" and then the commercial featured a Wendy's burger with extra-large, juicy patties of beef. It was one of the most successful ad campaigns in history.

I think of this woman's reaction when I go to the sub sandwich shop next to my office. Almost every time I go, this shop seems to be out of something. I can't tell you how many times I've ordered a sandwich only to find out while it is being made that the restaurant is out of pickles or tomatoes or onions. Because all these items contribute to my enjoyment of a good sub, I get very frustrated. I can understand a mega-sized home improvement store running out of quarter-inch wood screws, because it has a massive inventory to keep track of. But a sub shop's inventory isn't that complicated, so running out of pickles or tomatoes is a pretty big deal.

Then one day the sub experience hit an all-time low. I went to order a foot-long sandwich, and the employee told me, "Sorry. We're out of bread." Not just a specific kind of bread—they were completely out of bread. How do you respond to this? I tried to hide my shock and disgust as I said, "Let me get this straight. Your business is selling sandwiches, and you're out of bread?" To top it off, the employee condescendingly made me feel bad for being upset about this and told me I could order a low-carb wrap or come back in thirty minutes for bread. (I chose Door No. 3 and bought my lunch somewhere else.)

The more I thought about this, the more dumbstruck I was. A sub shop running out of bread is like a dairy farm running out of cows or a service station running out of gasoline or a chicken sandwich restaurant running out of chicken. Some items are staples that you can't do business without.

I believe many Christians today experience spiritual dilemmas like mine in the sub shop. They know that Jesus was a person of love, and they may even love and respect Jesus. But they walk into church or encounter someone who claims to know Christ and are left saying, "Where's the love? Where's the sacrifice?"

This is a huge problem for us as Christians. How can we claim to follow Christ if we are living in a way opposite to the values he demonstrated? If greed rules our hearts like it did Ananias and Sapphira's, we give the world a misrepresentation of our Savior. But Barnabas and the rest of the early church show us a different way in this passage. We can leave the vice of greed behind and experience freedom as we impact the world through sacrifice.

prayer exercise:

Examine your life and find something that you can give away to someone. Ask the Spirit of God to help you determine how big or small this sacrifice should be. Then, as an act of putting your prayer in action, make the small step of sacrifice and give this possession away. Enjoy this act of sacrifice and watch to see how it affects the people involved including you.

take me
from my life

Christmas was approaching, and I knew exactly what I wanted—a BMX bicycle. It was the most beautiful thing my nine-year-old eyes had ever seen. I wanted it so bad I couldn't see straight. I dreamed about the day that I would ride this beautiful machine up and down the streets of my neighborhood. As Christmas morning approached, I could hardly sleep from the excitement. I figured that my parents, my grandmother, or Santa Claus would come through and give me the present I longed for. But on December 25, there was no bicycle. I was absolutely devastated.

Before the day was over, I had moved to plan B on how to get my bicycle. I talked to my mom, and she said that if I saved enough money to pay half the price of the bike, she would pay the other half. I did chores for what seemed like forever to save this money. Many times, I hated doing those chores. I almost gave up every other day, but I kept at it. Finally, I had saved enough money for my half of the bike.

Sacrifice became real for me through that experience. When I rode that bike, I felt like a million dollars. It meant so much more to me because I had worked so hard and sacrificed so much to get it. If I had gotten that bike for Christmas, I would not have appreciated it nearly as much.

■ **What sacrifices have you made in your life?**

_____

_____

_____

_____

_____

Read Luke 1:26-38

■ What sacrifices do you think Mary had to make during this time in her life?

_____

_____

_____

_____

Fill in the blanks
Luke 1:38 says, "'I am the Lord's _____,' Mary answered. "May it _____ to _____ as you have _____.' Then the angel left her."

Most of us know this story about how the angel Gabriel came to tell a young girl named Mary that she would give birth to the Christ child. But we often overlook how much Mary willingly sacrificed as these events unfolded. According to verse 38, she acknowledged that her life was not her own and that God had the freedom to do whatever he wanted with her. She came to God on his terms, not on her own. This gives us a beautiful picture of what it means to sacrifice.

Many of us want to follow God on our terms instead of his. We want to call the shots in our lives to make sure that we get what we want, and thus we often turn up our noses at the thought of sacrifice. But it is in sacrifice that we find the life of freedom, the life that says, "Not as I will, but as you will," as Jesus did in Matthew 26:39.

prayer exercise:

Reread this passage and think about all the sacrifices that Mary had to make. Then look at your own life. Are you making sacrifices when God calls you to do so? Are you holding onto things out of greed instead of

sacrificing? Ask the Lord to use
this passage in Luke to show you
more about who he is and who he
wants you to be.

freedom
in sacrifice

John 13: 1-17

One of my favorite movies is *The Shawshank Redemption*. This movie tells the story of Andy Dufresne, who was wrongly convicted of committing murder. Most of the movie focuses on what life is like in prison (especially with a corrupt warden) and the hopelessness such a miserable existence brings. My heart always goes out to Andy as I watch him deal with the pain of being incarcerated for all the wrong reasons.

But Andy doesn't lose hope; he finds a way out. He gets a small rock pick through the prisoner black market and, over the years, slowly tunnels through the prison wall. He successfully escapes, and every time I watch the movie I celebrate his hard-won freedom. The movie gives us a great picture of redemption and hope coming through a long sacrifice.

■ What do you think freedom in the Christian life looks like?

_____

_____

_____

■ Do you feel like you walk in freedom?
   ❏ yes
   ❏ no

Why or why not?

_____

_____

_____

_____

Jesus was a master at turning the tables on his disciples. He often blew their minds with the way he looked at things. This story is another example of this, as Jesus took on the role of a servant and washed the feet of his disciples.

The more you read the Bible, the more you see how Jesus looks at things differently than we do. We may think that freedom means a cushy, easy life without any worries. But when Jesus washed his disciples' feet and told them to do the same, he was showing them the real way to freedom—through sacrifice. There is so much joy and purpose in a life lived this way. Andy Dufresne cherished his freedom because it came through such a sacrifice of time, energy, and effort.

We are wired to want to receive, but Jesus tells us that it is more blessed to give than to receive. Our greedy flesh cries out for more stuff, but our souls long for the freedom that can only be found in sacrifice. The challenge is turning our back on the way the world does things and venturing out into the life of sacrifice. Sadly, few find this kind of kingdom life. But Jesus told us that would happen. The road to sacrifice is the narrow way, but it is the way to freedom.

- How do you think the disciples found freedom in becoming men of generosity and sacrifice?

_____

_____

_____

- How have you found freedom in becoming a person who gives and sacrifices?

_____

_____

_____

Take some time to sit quietly before the Lord and let him speak to you. Ask him to give you the ability to hear him. Just like any good Father, he wants and desires to speak to you and lead you to the best life. Ask him to give you the ability to find freedom in sacrifice.

_____

_____

_____

_____

_____

_____

_____

_____

_____

_____

_____

_____

_____

_____

   This page is designed to give you space to take notes during your "Vice Versa" group session or to journal your reflections on the highlights of this week's study.

WEEK SIX

from gluttony to trust
(God is enough for tomorrow)

daily
bread

I've heard a lot of sermons in my life. In fact, if you counted up every sermon I've ever heard and gave me a dollar for each one, I'd have enough money to buy a really nice car. But I have never heard a sermon on gluttony.

- **What is your definition of gluttony?**

_____

_____

_____

We don't really like to talk about gluttony in our culture. On the rare times we do discuss it, we usually associate gluttony with food, because that's the textbook definition: excess in eating or drinking. But gluttony is not just about food and drink; it's about over-consumption of anything. That's an issue with which all of us in the United States can identify. Our nation is perhaps the biggest consumer in the history of the world. This week, we're going to look at gluttony and try to discover the freedom from over-consumption that God wants us to experience.

Read Exodus 16

The story of how God delivered his people from slavery in Egypt is a dramatic account of hope and triumph. The Israelites were oppressed by Pharaoh, and they desperately wanted freedom. God heard his people's cries and came to the rescue. He led them through a parted Red Sea and guided them toward the Promised Land. During the Israelites' trek through the wilderness, God promised he would provide for their needs by sending a food called **manna**. As you just read, they were to gather this food each day.

Well, some of them gathered more than they could eat in one day. This is a great example of gluttony. With their actions, they were saying, "There might not be enough manna tomorrow. I'm going to get all I can now." They didn't trust God and his provision for them. Because they had to pick up manna once a day, the Israelites had to learn to trust God on a daily basis. That trust is what God desired from them.

The vice of gluttony is essentially a problem with trust. By over-consuming, we show that we don't trust our heavenly Father. As we look at gluttony this week, ask yourself where you are in your trust level with the Lord.

■ Would you have gathered more than your daily bread if you were an Israelite?

❑ yes
❑ no

Why or why not?

_____

_____

_____

■ How do you struggle with trusting God in your life?

_____

_____

_____

prayer exercise:

Ask the Lord to open your eyes to what gluttony is and how it involves so much more than food. Spend some time reflecting on this passage and ask God to show you any places in your life where your actions demonstrate a lack of trust.

the
temptation for more

At the core of gluttony, as well as most of the other sins we are looking at, is a fundamental element of distrust. For some reason, I picture gluttony as a chubby little garden gnome. If you don't know what a garden gnome is, picture an elf that is 20 pounds overweight and holding a pipe. This gluttony gnome is how I picture the voice inside all of us that says, "Get more while you can, or someone else will take it."

A glutton is not just someone who eats too much. It's someone who hoards anything that could bring them pleasure. Today we're going to look at Achan, whose story gives us a vivid picture of gluttony.

Read Joshua 7

■ How is stealing a form of gluttony?

_____

_____

_____

■ Have you ever had anything stolen from you?
- ❑ yes
- ❑ no

If so, how did it make you feel?

_____

_____

_____

When you first read this story, you may wonder what the big deal is. So what if Achan took some extra loot from a city the Israelites had defeated—

he was taking it from Israel's enemies, wasn't he? But let's put the story in context. The Israelites had just crossed the Jordan River and entered the Promised Land after wandering around the desert for forty years because they didn't trust God. When they came to the city of Jericho, God told them to use the strangest military tactic ever conceived—marching around the city with a band instead of an army. The Israelites trusted God, and the walls of Jericho came crashing down. As they overtook the city, the Israelites collected all the best stuff for the treasury of the Lord's house and celebrated the benefits of trusting God. But as Achan helped haul out this national treasure—which was going to the treasury to help provide for all the Israelites, including Achan—he decided that, instead of trusting God, he should skim a little off the top for himself. Instead of trusting God for everything he needed, Achan listened to the gluttony gnome that told him to get more.

■ What did Achan steal, according to verses 20-21?

_____

_____

■ What good did those things do Achan?
- ❑ They made him the best-dressed Israelite.
- ❑ They paid for a new tent and a top-of-the-line camel.
- ❑ They allowed him to give more money to the poor.
- ❑ They were untouched, buried in the dirt underneath his tent.

■ What did Achan's actions cost the nation of Israel, according to verses 4-5?

_____

_____

_____

- In what areas of life are you tempted to listen to the gluttony gnome?

_____

_____

_____

- How could gluttony in those areas affect you and those around you?

_____

_____

_____

_____

prayer exercise:

Ask God to continue to show you areas in your life that are infected with the temptation for more. Confess these areas to him and ask him for the courage to move from distrust to trust in these areas.

the
generosity of God

When I was in the seventh grade, something happened in one of my classes that I'll never forget. One of my teachers cared about all his students, and we loved him dearly. I can remember how I actually enjoyed going to his class, and that says a lot for a seventh-grader. His class was fun, and I was never worried about being embarrassed in any way when I asked a question. He created an atmosphere of trust that allowed all of us to learn.

But in the middle of the school year, I walked into his classroom only to find another teacher there. I figured that she must be a substitute, but I quickly found out that she would be our teacher for the rest of the year. The teacher we loved and trusted had to leave for medical reasons, and we were left with a teacher whom none of us knew. The level of trust between this teacher and the students was very different than before. Without that trust, I wasn't able to learn in the same way I had under my old teacher. I don't think I raised my hand the rest of the year, because the new teacher was not afraid to make someone feel small if that person asked a silly question. Without any trust, I retreated into a shell and went through the motions of learning.

■ Do you have a hard time trusting God?

❑ yes
❑ no

If so, why do you think that this is?
If not, why not?

_____

_____

_____

_____

■ Why do you think so many people have a hard time trusting God?

_____

_____

_____

_____

Read John 10:7-10

Fill in the blanks
In John 10:10, Jesus says, "The
_____ comes only to _____ and
_____ and _____; I have come
that they may have _____, and have
it to the _____."

As we've already seen this week, gluttony is basically telling God that we don't trust him. Gluttony leads us to hoard things—including but not only food—because we don't think there will be enough to go around. It's closely related to the issue of greed we talked about last week, because many people have a hard time giving money away to those in need because they don't think there will be enough left for them to have everything they want and need.

The root problem with the vice of gluttony is in our view of God. If I think that God is out to get me, then I am going to have a pretty hard time trusting him. But this verse in John says that God wants us to experience life to the full. God is not the one on the prowl looking to destroy us any way he can. Jesus came to set people free, not to steal their lives away.

When we get a picture of who our generous God really is, we see that we can trust him with our lives. But if we constantly doubt the goodness of God, we're not going to be inclined to trust him. If you are struggling with gluttony and over-consumption, you need to ask yourself if you truly trust him with your life. Many times, we gorge ourselves on things because we don't trust the Father to provide those things. But our God is generous, and he is worthy of our trust.

Use this time of prayer to thank Jesus for coming to give us life to the full. Ask him to identify any areas in your life where a lack of trust is keeping you from receiving this kind of life from him. Ask him to help you see him for who he really is a loving, generous Father.

choosing
trust

■ If you could ask God for anything, what would you ask for?

_____

_____

_____

_____

Read 1 Kings 3:1-15

Fill in the blanks
In 1 Kings 3:9, Solomon says, "So give your servant a _____ _____ to govern your people and to distinguish between _____ and _____. For who is able to govern this great people of yours?"

I can't imagine what I would say if God told me he would give me whatever I asked for. It's even harder to imagine answering that question in Solomon's shoes. He had taken over for his father David, the most successful king Israel ever had, as the leader of God's people. He could have asked for the military success his father had, or for the temple his father wanted to build but couldn't, or for wealth that could provide for all of his and his nation's needs and wants.

But Solomon didn't ask for any of these things. His request was for wisdom and a discerning heart. Solomon had an unbelievable opportunity for gluttony here. He could have asked for anything he wanted to consume. But instead, he trusted God enough that he didn't ask for possessions but for wisdom.

- **What is remarkable about Solomon's request for a discerning heart?**

_____

_____

_____

_____

If you read the rest of 1 Kings, you'll see that Solomon was not a perfect person. He made mistakes, just like all of us do. But the thing that we remember most about him is this encounter with God. As we go on our journeys with Jesus, we have to make decisions every single day. We can either choose to hoard things to consume, or we can choose to trust. God's hope for us is clear. His best comes when we trust that he will give us what we need and therefore let go of the things we are grasping and hoarding.

- **Would you have asked God for wisdom as Solomon did?**
    - ❑ yes
    - ❑ no

Why or why not?

_____

_____

_____

- **What are some practical ways you can choose trust instead of gluttony today?**

_____

_____

_____

Write a letter to the Lord that expresses your desire to be a person who trusts him and not a person driven by over-consumption. Ask him to help you walk in the Spirit instead of always giving in to the desires of your flesh. Tell him that you trust him to give you the courage to live this way.

_____

_____

_____

_____

freedom
in trust

As I sit at my desk on a rainy morning, trying desperately to find the words to encourage you about the freedom in trust that God offers, I realize that I need the same encouragement. It's quiet in the office as our team of writers plies its craft, but I can hear knocking. Banging at the door of my brain is a ruthless band of control freaks all screaming for my attention. I am responsible for these gluttons of distrust. I feed them with worry, anxiety, and nervousness in an attempt to keep them quiet, but doing so only raises the volume of their accusations. *You'd better hurry up so that you meet your deadline.... Do you really think anyone is going to read this garbage?... When are you going to get ready for the retreat you're speaking at this weekend?... You need to spend more time with your family.... You don't make enough money, and you're never going to get out of debt.... Where is your life going?*

I wish I could say these thoughts are just normal, because living in the real world with adult responsibilities will produce a little stress. But these gluttonous voices were there when I was a student too; they just used different words. *You'd better hurry up and finish your homework, or you're going to fail again.... You need to get a girlfriend, because your social life is in the toilet.... Your part-time job stinks, and you have no idea what you want to do with your life.... Where is your life going?*

Gluttony is ultimately about control. Although I'm not obese, I know what it's like to get fat with comfort and complacency. Although I'm not a substance abuser, I know what it's like to abuse pleasure and put my needs above all else. Although I'm not rich, I know what it's like to be greedy and materialistic. And although I'm a Christian who loves Jesus, I know what it's like not to trust him.

- Take a moment to list anything that is competing for your attention right now.

_____

_____

_____

_____

Now go through the list and one by one, ask God to take those things away.

Did they go away? Chances are that, even though God grants you his peace, all your concerns won't disappear with the wave of a hand or one whispered prayer. The beauty of relentless trust is not that it magically takes away all our problems or concerns. Instead, trust is allowing God to do his job as Lord. Trust is getting off the throne of your heart and asking God to take his seat again. That's why there is so much freedom in childlike trust that believes and hopes that God's love for us will bring purpose and meaning in our lives for his Kingdom.

A friend of mine named Keith Miller often compares the freedom found in a relentless trust in God to a trapeze act. When you go to the circus and see the trapeze artists, you don't want to see them just climb a high platform and stand there. Chills don't run down your spine if they get on the bar fifty feet above the ground and swing back and forth. You go to see someone risk it all in trust. A trapeze artist believes with all his heart that, when he lets go of the bar and flies high above the ground at exhilarating speeds, at the last possible moment another swing will appear, and someone will be there to grab him and keep him safe. Trust put into action like this is breathtaking. While suffering on the cross, Jesus trusted the Father in an even more breathtaking way so that we could live in the freedom of trusting God.

Read Luke 23:46

■ Which best describes your journey of trusting God?

- ❏ I'm standing on the platform, unsure and afraid.
- ❏ I'm swinging on the trapeze, but I'm too scared to let go.
- ❏ I'm hanging in mid-air, holding God with one hand and clinging to my trapeze with the other.
- ❏ I'm soaring fearlessly in the air.
- ❏ I'm bouncing on the safety net, ashamed of having fallen.

prayer exercise:

Go back to the list you made earlier in this devotion. Pray the prayer Jesus prayed on the cross about each item on the list: "Father, into your hands I commit _____." Whenever you hear the gluttonous voices today, whisper this prayer again.

_____

_____

_____

_____

_____

_____

_____

_____

_____

_____

_____

_____

_____

    This page is designed to give you space to take notes during your
"Vice Versa" group session or to journal your reflections on the highlights
of this week's study.

VICE VERSA

WEEK SEVEN

from anger to gentleness
(learning to let go)

VICE VERSA: FROM ANGER TO GENTLENESS

anger
in action

When I was a senior in high school, I was traveling on Interstate 85 through Atlanta, Georgia. As I sat in rush-hour traffic, I looked to the right side of the road, and I saw something I couldn't believe. A woman was screaming at a man and beating him with a 2x4. I thought this must have been some sort of joke or prank at first, but after hearing this lady scream I realized she wasn't kidding. She said words I had never heard before in a display that looked like something out of a movie. I've never before seen and probably will never again see someone as angry as she was. She was taking out her frustrations on this man for everyone on I-85 to see.

- Do you struggle with anger?
  - ❑ yes
  - ❑ no

If so, what forms does your anger take?

_____

_____

_____

_____

- Why do you think so many people struggle with anger?

_____

_____

_____

- What is your definition of anger?

_____

_____

Read Acts 9:1-2

Fill in the blanks
Acts 9:1 says, "Meanwhile, Saul was still breathing out _____ _____ against the _____ _____."

We don't normally think about it, but the early accounts of the apostle Paul (originally known as Saul) show how he was a person of anger, rage, and hate. He abhorred followers of Jesus Christ, and he was out to get rid of them. In Acts 9, Paul had an encounter with Jesus that changed what he was like. He was still a sparkplug, yet he was known not as an angry crusader but as the apostle of grace.

When you look at our world, you see many angry people. If you don't believe me, spend some time in a car and notice road rage in action. This week we're looking at the vice of anger. We'll see how the gentleness of Jesus provides a stark contrast to the anger we so often see around us. Then we will think about whether there's anything we can do to deal with our anger.

- Why do you think anger is such a big deal to God?

_____

_____

_____

_____

_____

■ What are your goals this week as you think about moving from anger to gentleness?

_____

_____

_____

_____

prayer exercise:

Expectation plays an important role in our Christian lives. Take a moment and ask yourself if you really expect God to speak to you this week. Do you honestly believe that he wants to reveal himself to you? Expect to meet him this week. Expect to connect with him through this study of anger. Take some time now to open your heart to him. Talk to him about whatever is going on in your life and invite him to spend some time with you.

why are you so angry?

A friend of mine has a five-year-old nephew who is quite a character. Stephen always says exactly what he feels. Stephen was used to being the center of attention, so it's no surprise that he had a difficult time adjusting to the arrival of his new baby sister. When he got to his grandparents' house for Thanksgiving, Stephen couldn't understand why everyone was paying so much attention to the baby. Finally, he had enough and shouted, "Why is no one looking at me?"

Stephen's reaction is similar to how Joseph's older brothers felt. They could only watch as Joseph got all their father's attention and favor. Then one day, Joseph decided to tell them about a dream he had in which they all bowed down to him.

Read Genesis 37:18-20

■ Why do you think Joseph's brothers were so angry with him?

_____

_____

_____

■ Did they deal with their anger in a healthy way?

❑ yes
❑ no

What are some healthier ways they could have dealt with their anger?

_____

_____

Joseph's brothers had every right to be angry. Anger comes naturally to us. Sometimes anger is the appropriate reaction, as we'll see in tomorrow's devotion. But we can easily go wrong in how we express our anger. The downfall for Joseph's brothers was not being angry; it was failing to recognize why they were so angry with Joseph or how they should deal with that anger.

Anger is usually an expression of pain that we have difficulty coming to terms with. Joseph's brothers undoubtedly felt the pain of being overlooked and ignored by their father, in addition to the natural competition that exists between siblings.

We all deal with anger and pain in different ways, and if we are to move from anger to gentleness, we need to recognize how this process is at work in our lives. This may be a new step for you if you've heard that all anger is bad or that thinking about yourself is always selfish. Whatever your background, use the following questions to ask God's Spirit for wisdom as you examine your life.

- What things in your life cause you to be angry?

- Why are you angry? What is the pain behind your anger?

- How do you release your anger? (Check all that apply)
  - ☐ exercise
  - ☐ music
  - ☐ talking with friends
  - ☐ prayer
  - ☐ jokes
  - ☐ internalizing it
  - ☐ fighting
  - ☐ journaling
  - ☐ talking with parents
  - ☐ video games
  - ☐ picking on others
  - ☐ other _____

prayer exercise:

Ask God to continue revealing the pain in your life that is leading to anger. Ask him for wisdom in finding healthy ways to express your anger. Confess any places where God shows you that you are expressing your anger in inappropriate ways.

godly
anger

We think of many things when we try to describe Jesus—how he is gentle, loving, kind, and full of grace, truth, and compassion. But Jesus also shows us something in the Bible that catches many of us off-guard. Few of us would describe Jesus as angry, but in a few instances in the gospels, we see Jesus this way. Can you imagine a book called *The Angry Jesus*? As we seek to move from anger to gentleness, let's look at the truth about godly anger.

Read Matthew 21:12-17

■ **What made Jesus so angry in this passage?**

_____

_____

■ **Why do you think he reacted the way he did?**

_____

_____

_____

While he was on earth, Jesus had a relationship with his heavenly Father that we can hardly imagine. He constantly thought of the Father and told people how wonderful the Father truly is. God the Father became flesh in Jesus, and Jesus revealed what Father is truly like. Because of this intimate connection with the Father, Jesus knew what God was and was not like. That means that Jesus' expression of anger was Godly and holy.

When we look at Jesus' life, we see that he got angry at one set of people over and over. He had little patience with the religious establishment. In this passage, Jesus encounters people who had turned the temple into a kind of flea market. Jesus knew that God's intention for the temple (a house of prayer) and man's treatment of the temple (a den of robbers) were vastly different, and he got angry that God was being misrepresented.

It may seem strange that Jesus never showed this kind of anger to the outcasts, the downtrodden, the spiritually unclean, or even obvious sinners. Instead, he drew them to himself as they realized their need for a Savior. Jesus reserved his anger for the religiously arrogant and self-righteous.

One of the things we learn from this passage is that anger can be expressed in a healthy way, because Jesus did so. If a person is in bondage to the enemy, and we detect this, then we ought to burn in anger at that to which our friends have fallen prey. There's nothing wrong with having a godly anger toward the evil one and his ways. The challenge we face is learning how to have this godly anger without allowing our flesh to lash out at anything and everything. Getting angry and screaming at someone for cutting you off on in traffic is not the kind of anger Jesus displayed here.

- Is it possible for us to have a godly anger?
    - ❏ yes
    - ❏ no

Why or why not?

_____

_____

_____

- Have you ever experienced a godly kind of anger before?
    - ❏ yes
    - ❏ no

If so, explain that situation.

_____

_____

_____

- Why is it important for us to show godly anger? When is it important for us to do so?

_____

_____

_____

_____

_____

prayer exercise:

Ask the Lord to help you discern what it is like to express anger that honors him. Ask him to show you any situations in your life where you need to do so. Thank God for the example of Jesus when it comes to showing both gentleness and anger.

the
gentleness of Jesus

My grandmother is the sweetest person I have ever met. When I think about what it means to be gentle, I think of her. When I was growing up, my visits to my grandmother's house were the highlights of my year. If you've ever been around someone who is constantly gentle and loving, you know how valuable a relationship with that person is. Some of us can be gentle from time to time, but some people have a special gift of gentleness, and everyone who meets my grandmother describes her this way. Being in her presence is so calming that you don't ever want to leave.

But many of us misunderstand gentleness. Being gentle does not equal being weak. My grandmother is also a very strong person. When I was 7, I did an amazingly dumb thing. I threw a rock at a girl and hit her in the head. I didn't even have a reason or an excuse for doing it. Well, my grandmother caught me in the act. Most people would yell at a kid for doing something like that, but not my grandmother. She took me inside and calmly explained to me how wrong what I had done was. She told me that I had disappointed her, and that's all it took for me to start crying my eyes out. She cut me deep with her gentleness, and by being so gentle with me, she taught me one of the biggest lessons I ever learned.

■ **Why do we long to be around gentle people?**

_____

_____

_____

■ **Why is it so hard for us to be gentle?**

_____

_____

_____

Fill in the blanks

In John 8:11, Jesus said, "Then _____ do I _____ you. _____ now and _____ your life of _____. "

In Jesus' day, the religious establishment was known for many things, but gentleness was not one of them. The religious leaders were harsh, arrogant, and mean. In this story, we see how they treated a woman who had been caught in the act of adultery—a serious sin punishable in that time by death.

The way Jesus dealt with this woman was very different than the way the religious leaders did. They wanted to stone her, but Jesus wanted to forgive her. They wanted vengeance, but he wanted redemption. They wanted to express their anger, but he wanted to show gentleness.

The more I get to know Jesus, the more I am blown away by who he is. He showed anger at times, as we saw in Day Three. But the gentleness reflected in this passage is contagious. Christian tradition suggests that this woman was Mary Magdalene and that she completely changed after this encounter and became one of Jesus' most devoted followers. The gentleness of Jesus gave this woman freedom from her sin.

prayer exercise:

Celebrate the gentleness of Christ by sitting quietly before him. Take a few moments to bask in his presence and enjoy being with him.

VICE VERSA: FROM ANGER TO GENTLENESS

breaking
the cycle

Earlier this week, we looked at Joseph's brothers and saw how, while their anger was justified, the way they expressed it was very unhealthy. Now, as we seek to emulate the gentleness of Jesus that we thought about yesterday, we jump ahead in Joseph's story. Joseph's brothers sold him into slavery, dividing their family and causing Joseph to spend the next eighteen years in a foreign land as a slave and then a prisoner. Eventually, God put Joseph in a position of power and reunited him with his brothers, and Joseph had a chance to settle the score.

Read Genesis 50:14-21

- Are you surprised by Joseph's response?
  - ❑ yes
  - ❑ no

- What would you have done if you were in Joseph's place?

_____

_____

_____

Instead of lashing out, Joseph decided once and for all to break the cycle of anger in his family. He certainly had good reasons to be angry. (If you want to learn more of the story, go back and read Genesis 39—45.) Now, the dreams Joseph had as a young man—the same dreams that had fueled his brothers' anger and jealousy—had finally come true. Joseph had the chance for revenge. He could shout, "I told you! I told you!" and have his brothers imprisoned. But he resisted these urges.

A careful reading of the whole story shows us that Joseph couldn't resist messing with his brothers' heads and toying with their emotions. It would have been easy for him to continue to express his anger in big and small ways now that his father wasn't around to intervene. That's what his brothers were afraid would happen. But Joseph decided to restore his family and break the cycle of anger.

■ **Has anyone you hurt responded with gentleness instead of anger?**

❑ yes
❑ no

If so, how did that make you feel?

_____

_____

_____

■ **Have you ever responded gently to someone at whom you had the right to be angry?**

❑ yes
❑ no

If so, what happened after you did so?

_____

_____

_____

We get glimpses of courageous acts of gentleness in today's news and throughout history. People who have every right to be angry and demand justice instead respond with gentleness. The recipients of grace and observers alike are struck with the force of a tidal wave as the mercy of God floods over them.

- A man pleads in open court for mercy for the drunk driver who killed his wife and child.

- A Jewish woman offers forgiveness to her Nazi torturer when he walks into her church years after the Holocaust.

- A son seeks out and forgives his deadbeat father for abusing him and his mother and abandoning them to a life of poverty.

- A little black girl whispers prayers for the angry white men who spit on her and curse at her, as she becomes the first black student in her public elementary school.

- A student who is ridiculed by the "in" crowd at school welcomes a member of the clique who is visiting his youth group and has no one to sit with.

- A man whispers a prayer to forgive the angry people who are torturing him to death as he hangs on two wooden planks that form the shape of a cross.

prayer exercise:

Ask God to lead you from anger to gentleness as you answer the following questions.

- With whom are you trapped in the anger cycle right now?

_____

_____

- How can you break the anger cycle and reach out to these people in gentleness?

_____

_____

_____

_____

_____

_____

_____

_____

_____

_____

_____

_____

_____

_____

This page is designed to give you space to take notes during your "Vice Versa" group session or to journal your reflections on the highlights of this week's study.

WEEK EIGHT

freedom
(time to fly)

the gift
of grace

Welcome to the final week of *Vice Versa*. We hope and pray that you are experiencing God's gracious freedom as you wrestle with what Saint Augustine considered the most important thing in life—knowing God and knowing yourself. You have bravely gone to the depths of your soul to honestly see your own vices and have through Scripture and prayer seen the freedom God offers. Now let's take some time to (as Big Daddy Weave would say) dance with Father God in fields of grace.

■ What do you think of when you hear the word grace?

    ❏ something you say before a meal
    ❏ a girl's name
    ❏ an often-used church word
    ❏ a free gift

■ Describe grace in your own words.

_____

_____

_____

■ How have you experienced grace in your own life? Give two or three examples.

_____

_____

_____

_____

It's hard for us to imagine sometimes, but even when we struggle with the vices we've talked about in this book, God still considers us his workmanship. Think about it: God holds us up as his trophies, not because of anything we have done, but because of what he has done with us. When I struggle with the vices we've examined, I tend to get really mad at myself, and I'm tempted to try harder to pay God back for saving me. There are some days when I don't feel like I've earned the right to be God's child. My guess is that you've felt that way too.

But these verses tell us that we **never** earn the right to be God's children; it is **by grace** that we have been saved—not by anything we have done. God's grace is not only the basis for our relationships with Jesus; it is what keeps these relationships going. What a relief it is to realize that Jesus loves me just as I am right now—not as I should be or as I'm going to be. God's grace is always there for us; it's up to us to choose to accept and unwrap this gift every day of our lives.

■ **What is the best gift you have ever given someone?**

_____

_____

■ **How did that person respond to that gift?**

_____

_____

Can you imagine giving someone a birthday or Christmas gift at a party only to discover that the recipient never unwraps it? The recipient enjoys the beautiful wrapping paper, says thank you and tells everyone how thoughtful you are, but at the end of the party gives back the gift and quietly tells you that he or she has not been a good enough friend to merit such a token of affection. Of course, this would be crazy.

But this is what we often do with God's free gift of grace. Instead of dancing around the room and telling everyone how good God is to us, we think that God's grace isn't good enough for those of us who struggle with sin. The truth that this study has shown us is that the only reason any of us have the courage to scratch away our polished exteriors and take an honest look at some of the sins we all deal with is that we know God's grace, mercy, and love cover us every second of the day. God's grace is the foundation for the freedom in Christ that we are chasing after, so let's rip open the gifts and get out on the dance floor.

prayer exercise:

- In what areas of your life is it difficult for you to accept God's grace?

_____

_____

_____

As you are honest with God and with yourself about this question, ask God to show you how his grace is for you even in your weakest moments and darkest places. You may want to listen to a worship CD to help this truth flood over you today.

the
ripple effect

Luke
5:17 25

Needing a break from the relentless pace of school, work, and ministry, I decided to take a silent retreat and go camping in the woods for a couple of days. One morning, as I was hiking and praying, I came across a hidden pond. The morning fog was lifting, and steam rose from the glassy surface of the water. I felt as though I was standing in a sanctuary. I approached the reflective edge of the pond with great reverence, drinking in the beauty as the morning rays of light danced through the evergreen trees.

This spiritual moment was followed in the next moment by a huge KER-PLUNK echoing through the silent forest. I stood there with a silly grin on my face after launching a five-pound rock into the previously undisturbed waters of this hidden pond. The bullfrogs started croaking, as if they were saying, "Pipe down! We're trying to sleep!" I know that I could have been still in that moment, but I couldn't resist throwing a rock into the water and then sitting back to watch the ripples.

When we jump headfirst into the depths of God's unwavering grace, we should expect to create ripples that affect the people around us. When we immerse ourselves in the freedom of God's gracious and unconditional acceptance, it always affects those around us. And by the way, splashing is allowed.

Read Luke 5:17-25

- What stands out to you about this story?
    - ❏ Jesus calling out the Pharisees
    - ❏ Jesus healing the paralyzed man
    - ❏ the willingness of the paralyzed man's friends to do whatever it took for him to find healing

- Have you ever had friends like this man had?
    - ❏ yes
    - ❏ no

If so, who are they?

_____

_____

- Have you ever been the kind of friend
  who says, "Just show me the corner
  and I'll carry it"?
    ❑ yes
    ❑ no

If so, explain that situation.

_____

_____

_____

Once you find freedom and healing in Jesus, your life will never be the same. People whom you would normally look down on or judge—the outcasts and those who don't have their act together—become the very people you are drawn to help. You will create a community of people who want live, love, and heal together, a community that doesn't hesitate to find a corner to carry, a community of the ripple effect.

Just before a youth-group meeting at an inner-city church in Boston, Yolanda slipped her hand up and asked if she could share something. The teacher said of course, but then Yolanda just fidgeted in her chair for a moment, to the point where the other children started to get restless. Finally, she said softly, "You know that my father has been missing." Tears began to well up in her eyes, and it was obvious that she was having trouble getting the words out. "They dragged him out of the Cooper River yesterday afternoon. He's dead." Little Yolanda bowed her head and began to shake uncontrollably with grief. The seal had been broken, the pressure released, the pain exposed, the anger uncovered. Yolanda had finally been able to share the immense burden she had shouldered alone for the past day.

Some of the other students came forward to put their arms around Yolanda, and others began to pray for her. When the prayers ended, Yolanda sat down with her youth minister and cried and cried. Her moans and wails echoed through the halls, creating a much different atmosphere than on most Monday nights at this church. The other students tried to sing as they usually did at their meetings, but Yolanda's sobbing almost drowned out their voices. Yet, as her wails met their songs, a remarkable sound was born. The pain Yolanda had expressed drove the rest of the students to sing more deeply and more honestly from their souls. And their songs united the community around the weeping girl. Yolanda's gentle, broken spirit was protected and embraced by friends who mourned with her, and everyone there experienced the freedom of love, of humility, of gentleness, and of blessing.

prayer exercise:

Ask God to show you those in your life who need you to pick up a corner for them. Take some time in silence to think about how God would have you do so. Then think about your own life and the places where you need someone to pick up a corner for you. Confess these areas to God and ask him to bring people into your life who can unleash the ripple effect.

virtue
from vice

2 Corinthians
12:9-10

Yesterday we talked about the ripple effect and how grace in our lives impacts others. The next step is for us to become leaders. Once we have dealt with the vices and sins that ensnare us and experience freedom, we should point others along the same path.

I was reading a leadership journal the other day and saw the story of a student named Simon. Simon decided to get serious about his relationship with God, so he signed up for a discipleship course with some of his buddies. Simon was the kind of guy everyone loved to be around. He was outspoken; he embraced responsibility; and he was always looking for opportunities to show his teacher his enthusiasm and loyalty to God. But very soon the teacher and the other students in Simon's class began to see some serious vices come to the surface in Simon's life. As the weeks went on, the teacher had to constantly tell Simon to stop speaking out of turn and to watch his bragging, and he frequently had to pull Simon aside when he failed to apply what they were studying. Even though Simon kept telling everyone about the amazing ministry he was going to start after he completed this discipleship class, no one was surprised when he dropped out in the final weeks of that class.

This story is all too familiar in our churches and youth group, and as we come to the end of this study, we need to think about how we can continue in the growth we have experienced in the past eight weeks.

■ **What do you feel are your strongest gifts, talents, desires, and areas of interest and compassion as a disciple of Jesus?**

_____

_____

_____

_____

■ What do you feel are your biggest weaknesses and struggles as a disciple of Jesus?

_____

_____

_____

_____

Read 2 Corinthians 12:9-10

■ As you look at your list of weaknesses, how do you think God's power can be made perfect in your weakness?

_____

_____

_____

_____

I always want God to make his power perfect or complete in my strengths, not my weaknesses. I grew up thinking the whole goal of the Christian life was to stop sinning, to terminate every weakness, and to do only good things all the time. At the end of the day, I measured my success as a believer not by God's grace and the sacrifice of love made by Jesus but by whether my strengths outweighed my weaknesses. But I've learned the same thing that Paul did: that kind of life is slavery, not freedom.

Let's return to the story of Simon, the uncommitted and wavering Christian. He ultimately came back and started an incredible ministry. Why? Because his teacher saw past his weaknesses, his struggles, and his vices and saw his potential, gifting, and virtue. Buried deep inside what appeared to be Simon's vices—his loud mouth, his arrogance, and his lack of commitment—were the gifts of leadership, passion, and intensity. Simon launched an incredible teaching and preaching ministry that his teacher put him in charge of. If Simon had only concentrated on getting rid of his weakness and struggles, he never would have unearthed the fact that they hid his true gift and calling. His vices disguised his virtues.

There's great freedom in serving a Savior who loves us both in our strengths and weaknesses. From the very beginning Jesus saw the virtues in Simon, which is why he named him Peter, which means "rock." Christ clearly intended for Peter to provide rock-solid leadership for the church. You can read all about Simon's dynamic preaching and teaching ministry in Luke's leadership journal, also known as The Book of Acts.

■ Take another look at your list of vices, struggles, and weaknesses. What virtues may be hidden beneath them?

_____

_____

_____

_____

prayer exercise:

Confess your vices to God and ask him to allow his power to be made perfect in your weakness. Praise God for loving you even in your weakness and celebrate his ability to bring virtue out of your vices.

2 Corinthians
5:21

assuming
your identity

■ List three things that you consider
critical parts of your identity.

_____

_____

_____

One of the great loves of my life was a two-foot-tall, fifty-five-pound, chubby English bulldog named Albus. He was a fat, lazy, ugly, stinky, snoring machine that I loved because he made me look neat by comparison. His favorite thing to do was to ride in the sidecar of my motorcycle. His chest bowed up with pride when he did, because he was hanging out with his papa. (Please forgive the cheesy dog-lover lingo.)

Albus had good days and bad days. On the good days, he was the perfect dog—gentle, affectionate, and well mannered. But on the bad days, he could be aggressive, disobedient, and stubborn. On the good days, I never doubted that the dog in front of me was my Albus. But on the bad days, I wondered whether this was really my Albus.

Regardless of his behavior, Albus' true identity was sealed the day I went to the breeder, picked him out of the litter, held him in my arms, and chose to take him home with me. From the moment I bought Albus, he was mine, and nothing would ever change that.

Jesus has redeemed us to set us free. **Redeemed** means paid for and bought back. Freedom in Christ is about recognizing this identity. The gospel of Jesus—the good news—is that no matter who we are, he is willing to adopt us as his children. Nothing will ever change our new identity.

Read 2 Corinthians 5:21

■ How did Jesus ransom or redeem us?

_____

_____

_____

_____

■ How does this verse describe us, in light of Jesus' payment?

_____

_____

_____

Jesus didn't just die on the cross so that we could get rid of some of the vices in our lives and replace them with a few more virtues. He died so that his perfect virtue would apply to us. He paid the full price for our sin and changed our entire identity. We have been adopted into the family of God, and nothing can ever take that identity away. We have been set free to become who we already are in God's eyes. We are in his sidecar for life, so hang on and enjoy the ride.

■ Describe the time in your life when you felt closest to God.

_____

_____

_____

_____

■ Describe a time in your life when you felt far away from God.

_____

_____

_____

- How does what God says about our
  identity change the way you look at
  those times?

_____

_____

_____

- Is there anything in your life right
  now that is not in keeping with your
  true identity in Christ?

_____

_____

_____

prayer exercise:

Ask God to give you a holy dissat-
isfaction with anything that hinders you from becoming who you
already are in his eyes. Thank him
for paying the price for your
righteousness.

time
to fly

Read Isaiah 61:1-3

Fill in the blanks
Isaiah 61:1-3 says, "The Spirit of the Sovereign LORD is on me, because the LORD has anointed me to preach _____ _____ to the _____. He has sent me to _____ up the _____, to proclaim _____ for the _____ and _____ from _____ for the _____, to _____ the year of the _____ _____ and the day of _____ of our God, to _____ all who _____, and _____ for those who _____ in Zion to bestow on them a _____ of _____ instead of _____, the oil of _____ instead of _____, and a garment of _____ instead of a spirit of _____. They will be called oaks of _____, a planting of the _____ for the display of his _____."

The purpose of this extended fill-in-the-blanks section is to help you comb through the power of this statement about our Lord's purpose. We saw in Week Three, that Jesus took this statement as his mission statement, as recorded in Luke 4. Jesus knew why he was here on earth and what he was to do. He is the healer, forgiver, deliverer, redeemer, and friend. He came to destroy the works of Satan and give us freedom.

This book has been all about freedom. We should never be satisfied with being stuck in the misery and bondage of our vices. To the proud, Jesus says there is freedom in humility. To the lustful, he says there is freedom to love. To the slothful, he says there is freedom in passion. To the envious, he says there is freedom to bless. To the greedy, he says freedom comes through sacrifice. To the gluttonous, he says there is freedom in trust. And to the angry, Jesus says there is freedom in gentleness.

With God, all things are possible, and he is still in the business of setting people free. The problem comes when we don't know how to receive the freedom that has already been purchased. The work is completed; Jesus told us as much on the cross when he said, "It is finished."

Whatever the vices you find yourself in bondage to, freedom is available. The Holy Spirit lives inside of you and is more than capable of leading you to freedom. The same power that raised Christ from the dead is inside us; now it is up to us to claim this power and ask the Spirit to lead us to freedom. Our Lord paid everything so that we can be free. He is the most compassionate, sacrificing friend we could ever ask for. As you complete this study today, dare to reach out to the Savior and give him whatever vices are in your life right now. He is able and willing to help you—whatever your situation. He is a God of freedom.

■ **Where have you experienced freedom in this study?**

_____

_____

_____

_____

■ **In what areas of your life do you still long to experience freedom?**

_____

_____

_____

_____

One of the best images of freedom is a caged bird being released to fly away. Birds reflect God's majesty as they float on wind currents and soar through the skies. The freedom birds experience in flight is immeasurably better than a stagnant life spent in a cage. God has created us to fly too. We hope this book has helped you to leave the cages of your vices so that you can live the life of freedom for which God created you. End this study by asking the Holy Spirit to help you remember the things you have learned over the past eight weeks. Thank God for being a God of freedom. Celebrate the work of freedom Jesus did on the cross. Meditate on the sacrifice Jesus made so that you can be free. Commit to being courageous to follow Christ in the freedom he sets before you. It's time to fly.

_____

_____

_____

_____

_____

_____

_____

_____

_____

_____

_____

_____

_____

   This page is designed to give you space to take notes during your
"Vice Versa" group session or to journal your reflections on the highlights
of this week's study.

About the Authors

CHAD NORRIS

Chad is a speaker and writer who desires to lead people in their spiritual journeys to become loving followers of Jesus Christ. In this calling, he speaks to children, students, and adults in a variety of settings and writes several resources. Chad is a co-founder of Wayfarer Ministries and serves as one of the weekly teachers for Engage, a praise and worship Bible study for 20-somethings in upstate South Carolina. After graduating from the University of Georgia in 1995, Chad received his Master of  Divinity from Beeson Divinity School in 2000. Chad's love of the journey and realistic viewpoints help nurture people in their personal spiritual growth. This is the fifth book Chad has co-authored in the Following God for Youth series. Chad, wife Wendy, and son Sam live in Greer, South Carolina.

DAVID RHODES

As a speaker and author, David has a passion to help people rediscover life as followers of Jesus Christ. His creative, challeng-  ing, and honest approach encourages a variety of individuals and groups in various ministry settings. David is a co-founder of Wayfarer Ministries and one of the weekly speakers at Engage, a praise-and-worship Bible study for 20-somethings in upstate South Carolina. David graduated from Palm Beach Atlantic University in 1996 and earned his Master of Divinity from Beeson Divinity School in 2000. This is the fifth book David has co-authored in the Following God for Youth series. David, wife Kim, and daughter Emma live near Greenville, South Carolina.

CHRIS BROOKS

Chris brings a contagious excitement for being a student of God's word and personifying its teaching within the context of commu-nity. Chris's holistic approach allows him to voice with humor and seriousness the cost of disciple-ship and to ask the hard questions that living the Christian life demands. Chris earned his Master of Divinity from Beeson Divinity School and spent six years as a producer, writer, and performer with Student Life before joining Wayfarer Ministries in 2004. He now serves as  one of the weekly speakers at Engage, a praise-and-worship experi-ence for 20-somethings in upstate South Carolina and also travels to speak to students of all ages at churches, camps, retreats, and other ministry settings. Chris, wife Audrey, and son Simon live in Spartanburg, South Carolina.

For more information about the authors of this study, please contact:
Wayfarer Ministries
116 Hidden Hill Road
Spartanburg, SC 29301
www.wayfarerministries.org

Other books in the
FOLLOWING GOD FOR YOUTH SERIES
Youth Curriculum Throughout the Year!

EACH BOOK IS AUTHORED BY DAVID RHODES AND CHAD NORRIS, CO-FOUNDERS OF WAYFARER MINISTRIES. WAYFARER IS A MINISTRY ON THE CUTTING EDGE OF TEACHING AND TRAINING YOUNG PEOPLE FOR CHRIST.

God Is...Exploring the Many Sides of God
Pondering the unfathomable attributes of God triggers many questions such as:

How can God be both huge and personal?
How can God be both holy and gracious?
How can God be both jealous and our Father?
How can God be both ordinary and mysterious?

God Is... examines some of the attributes of God, paradoxes and all, and explores what these attributes can mean in your life. Each day's reading will challenge your view of God.
168 pages **(ISBN:089957732-6)**

Dismantled: An Honest Look at Some of Our Biggest Fears
Walk down the road of Following God—in spite of your fears!

Lessons in Dismantled center on Bible characters who dealt with the issue of fear. Filled with practical applications that lead us "directly to the shelter of the Almighty, where fear has no power over us."
168 pages **(ISBN:089957734-2)**

LEADER'S GUIDES AND OTHER ESSENTIALS AVAILABLE
FOR ALL FIVE BIBLE STUDIES!!
Visit www.wayfarerministries.org
To order call: 1-800-266-4977 or log on to
www.amgpublishers.org

Other books in the
FOLLOWING GOD FOR YOUTH SERIES
Youth Curriculum Throughout the Year!

EACH BOOK IS AUTHORED BY DAVID RHODES AND CHAD
NORRIS, CO-FOUNDERS OF WAYFARER MINISTRIES.
WAYFARER IS A MINISTRY ON THE CUTTING EDGE OF
TEACHING AND TRAINING YOUNG PEOPLE FOR CHRIST.

Redefining Normal: Waking Up to Life as God Intends It

What is normal? For many of us, normal Christianity is
comfortable and secure, isolated and based on all the evils
that we don't do. But what if our norm isn't normal to God?

Redefining Normal challenges students to re-examine the
norm in both culture and and Christianity. Students will be
"turned upside down" as they examine the kind of people
God wants us to become. The challenge for young people in
this study is not just that they should live within God's
moral boundaries but that they will become people of
greater faith, hope, and love.

168 pages (**ISBN:089957736-9**)

Broken: When Life Falls Apart

Brokenness....Nobody wants it, yet most of us experience it.
What are we supposed to do when life crashes down
around us? Why does God allow his people to suffer?

Broken is an honest look at the life of Job and the lessons
it teaches us about what it means to follow God when life
falls apart. The study addresses the real-life pain and suffering we face and examines how we can trust God in the
midst of it as Job did.

160 pages (**ISBN:089957738-5**)

LEADER'S GUIDES AND OTHER ESSENTIALS AVAILABLE
FOR ALL FIVE BIBLE STUDIES!!
Visit www.wayfarerministries.org
To order call: 1-800-266-4977 or log on to
www.amgpublishers.org

notes

notes

notes

notes

notes